PRAISE FOR REHAB IS NOT FOR THE SOUL

It's a ride through the dark side, filled with the pain and hopelessness of addiction. From his own personal darkness, Gary reveals the steps that will bring you from the pit of bondage into true and lasting freedom…It's a must-read book written not just for people struggling with addictions, but also for family and friends who want to help.

SCOTT HOLMES
LIFE CHURCH, LEAD PASTOR SHREVEPORT, LOUISIANA

In this candid account of the destruction brought on by addiction and of the power of deliverance, Gary Bentley shares the ANSWER *for the addict today. A must-read for anyone plagued with addiction or dealing with family members who are addicts.*

TERESA BLAKNEY
SOUTHWESTERN ASSEMBLIES OF GOD UNIVERSITY

Gary's life story offers hope for every person, no matter how hopeless life may seem. His timeless stories and anecdotes help the reader understand what it's like to overcome fear, doubt, and life-controlling addictions. Gary Bentley's book is inspiring.

DOUG MCALLISTER
LEAD PASTOR—WWW.JOURNEYFELLOWSHIPCHURCH.COM

The old saying, "Been there, done that," holds true for author Gary Bentley, who has wonderful insight into secular treatment programs, codependency, enabling, biblical concepts of addiction and deliverance, and life free from addiction.

MIKE HODGES
TEEN CHALLENGE USA PRESIDENT (RETIRED)

God's unfathomable grace is on clear exhibition in Gary's experiences.... This is a wonderful book about a man who found grace to be more than just a word—it's a continuing walk!

DOUG FULENWIDER
SUPERINTENDENT
LOUISIANA DISTRICT ASSEMBLIES OF GOD

[Gary Bentley] is uniquely gifted in assisting others in finding their own personal place of freedom. I have witnessed his life and his ministry as he has helped untold hundreds of people find personal freedom.

PASTOR SHANE WARREN
THE ASSEMBLY, WEST MONROE, LOUISIANA
SHANE WARREN MINISTRIES

This amazing book has an amazing story about God's amazing grace... This book is a faith-builder for any reader.

CHRIS WITT
LEAD PASTOR, SOUTH PARKWAY CHURCH
RUSTON, LOUISIANA

In a day when everyone considers himself a "victim," Gary Bentley shows us that we are responsible for our decisions. Whether you are an addict, alcoholic, or neither, this book will point you to the greatest decision you are called to make—that is, the call of Jesus, to come to Him for the freedom only He can give.

PASTOR HAL WARREN
CALERA BAPTIST CHURCH
CALERA, ALABAMA

Gary Bentley brings a fresh and much-needed perspective to the area of alcohol and drug rehabilitation. ... More importantly Bentley identifies the key to true change comes through an emphasis on the spiritual dimension of a person's life. ... Bentley rightly concludes that only through this relationship and lifestyle, is there complete freedom for the addict.

DR. JACK SMART, PRESIDENT
TEEN CHALLENGE USA

Gary is a trophy of God's redeeming grace! There is hope and deliverance for you, too, through the power of the blood of Jesus and the anointing of the Holy Spirit.

PASTOR ANDY HARRIS
CENTRAL ASSEMBLY OF GOD
HAUGHTON, LOUISIANA

This is a wonderful book, full of insights into the freedom from addiction... Gary has great insight to the fallacy of the Twelve Step program and why so many fail at it. This is a must-read if you have a loved one who has been dealing with an addiction, and who has been through many treatment programs but to no avail. Gary will inspire you to ... believe your loved one can change.

GREG DILL
CEO, LOUISIANA TEEN CHALLENGE

REHAB IS NOT FOR THE SOUL:
A JOURNEY OUT OF ADDICTION

GARY BENTLEY

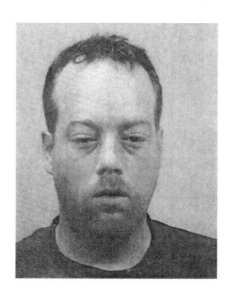

Bentley, Gary

Rehab Is Not for the Soul: A Journey Out of Addiction

ISBN: 978-0-9859281-0-0

Published by Bentley Books

Designed by Boyett Printing and Graphics

Edited by The Threepenny Editor

Page Layout by Phillip Gessert

Printed in the United States of America

Unless otherwise indicated, all biblical quotes herein are taken from the New American Standard Bible.

In memory of Randy "Little Red" Bentley

ACKNOWLEDGEMENTS

I would like to thank:

My wife Sandy, the love of my life and best friend. Thanks for working side-by-side with me in ministry.

My parents, Bobby and Annell Bentley, for their unconditional love and patience.

My brother, Matt—you are the best.

Reverend Greg Dill and his wife, Abigail Dill, for founding Greater New Orleans Teen Challenge, Inc. Without it, who knows.

CONTENTS

INTRODUCTION

I was on a mission trip to Russia fifteen years after I gave up drinking alcohol. I was there helping with a Leadership Training Institute for Global Teen Challenge. The last day of school, we had a special communion service. In Russia it is customary to use real wine, unlike in America, where we often use grape juice. The communion cup came my way; I drank it and immediately knew it was alcohol.

I felt the warm feeling in my chest, which I had once longed for as an alcoholic. Because I was a guest, my hosts brought me the wine that remained after everyone else was served. Not wanting to offend them, I drank it. The warm feeling got even warmer.

There are many people who are classified alcoholics and live their life sober, confessing that they will always be alcoholics. That trip to Russia confirmed what I have believed for fifteen years: that I am no longer an alcoholic. I am a new creation. There are many clinically diagnosed alcoholics whom the communion in Russia would have sent back to drinking. Were I not a new creation, I would have been in a bar in Moscow that night.

But that day in Russia, God showed me —as He has many times before—that I am free.

✝

re·ha·bil·i·tate

To restore formally to former capacity, standing, rank, rights, or privileges…

This is the definition of rehabilitation (Dictionary.com). It means to restore someone to what they once were. For anyone who is struggling with addiction, rehabilitation is the worst thing that could happen. He or she does not need to go back to a former state, rank, or privileges. A twenty-eight-year-old who needs help does not need to return to age twelve just to make the same decisions again. Something new needs to happen. That person needs to die and another one needs to take its place.

> *And I will give them one heart, and put a new spirit within them. And I will take the heart of stone out of their flesh and give them a heart of flesh, that they may walk in My statutes and keep My ordinances and do them. Then they will be My people, and I shall be their God.* (Ezekiel 11:19–20)

Rehab is for someone recovering from a stroke or knee injury, and trying to get his or her physical body back to its former state. Addicts around the world need a spiritual heart transplant. They need the heart that has been battered and made hard by the world replaced with a new heart that is soft and teachable. They need a heart that will follow after God.

The Problem

Over the years when I would think about the struggles I had with my life, the attempts to change my life and knowing the wonderful life that I have now, I would think about writing this book. Well, the thinking is over. I am now writing it in hope that not only the person who is addicted would benefit from it, but also his or her family and friends.

I want to encourage the reader, whoever you are, to read this book with an open heart and open mind. I can tell you this: My struggles and attempts to change are not a fairytale. They are for real, and what is even more real is the change that I am experiencing now. The change promises a life free from addictions, without having to go to meetings and share my struggles with a group of people. And not only am I free from addictions, but I have learned what real life is all about.

God was the author of this change. I know this statement will set some readers back. Maybe you are not a believer—maybe you are an agnostic, or maybe you just don't believe that God is working miracles today. That's normal, and that's why I will say it again: Please read this book with an open mind.

For years and years people have put God in a box, not thinking that He was the answer for certain problems, like addictions. Even believers have put their faith in secular treatment programs rather than in God. Well, I hope to change those minds as well.

This book is not a testimonial, but I share some of my struggles in order to help you through the dark times of addiction, whether you are the one addicted or the family member of someone who is. I talk about what went wrong for me, my attempts to stop my addictions through rehabilitation, and of course the change that came forth in my life. What's more important, I will spend a lot of time on how to enjoy your freedoms when you give your addictions to Jesus Christ—not God as you understand Him.

DOES THIS SOUND FAMILIAR?

HOW DID I GET HERE?

After a bout of drinking and cocaine abuse and two days in a detox wing, I was transferred to a semi-private room—a very nice room, as it should have been for a fee of $25,000, for twenty-eight days. This was in 1984. I was twenty-one and had checked into my first drug rehabilitation program.

I had been raised in church. I emphasize "raised in church." As a young adult, I never went to church because I wanted to and I never understood why I should. I may have been some sort of an agnostic—*one who is skeptical about the existence of God but does not profess true atheism.*

I think, deep down, I might have believed; but my life didn't reflect any sort of belief at all. Lying in this very expensive room reflecting on my future, I knew that I was on a really bad road. From the depths of my heart and soul I said the words. "God help me!" At that moment I experienced something that can only be described as a very light charge of electricity running through my body. I was at peace with myself and I felt like I had some hope.

Puzzled but excited about this experience, I went to my counselor the next morning and shared with him what had happened. He was nice and polite, but he referred me to the Catholic priest, who had gone through a secular treatment program for alcoholism. I was inspired by what had happened to me the night before, and I told the priest all about it. He looked at me and said, "What you had was an emotional experience, and you need to work the program. You are going to do well."

I looked up to him, and was going to listen to and put my faith in whatever he said. Because of experiences like this, which I will share more about later in the book, and the deliverance from my addictions, I wrote this book. As it turns out, it was not an emotional experience. That priest was wrong.

Peer Pressure

I can remember not being able to talk to girls as I was growing up. I was very shy. There was a girl in the fifth grade who passed me a note. She was one of the prettiest girls in the class. When I received it, I saw she'd confessed to liking me and wanted to sit with me during the assembly that afternoon. All I can remember was sitting there, terrified, and unable to even look her way. That moment was my window to be accepted by peers, and for whatever reason, that moment was a turning point for me. Word spread that Gary Bentley could not talk to girls.

What a devastating moment. As I look back, I believe it was important. My moment of insecurity turned me into the butt of jokes, and pushed my popular friends away. I had to start seeking acceptance elsewhere, and that is where the problem began.

Now don't misunderstand me. I wasn't a perfect child to begin with. I was guilty of the usual childish pranks, and the kind of adventures that parents lose sleep over—but my family would agree that I was basically a good kid. For a long time, I resisted peer pressure. There were nights walking around the neighborhood that I would be offered cigarettes, beer, or even pot. I turned it down many times. But, one night, it finally happened. I gave in.

The pressure of wanting to be accepted is real. I don't fully understand why it was so powerful for me; I often golfed with other friends, and we stayed out of trouble. Yet for some reason, I had to go elsewhere for acceptance. That's a mystery.

One night in our neighborhood, a few of us put our change together so we could cross the highway to Dobson's Grocery and get some Malt Duck. Of course we fought over who was going to actually go into the store and buy the alcohol, because this was the neighborhood store and we didn't want our parents to find out. Every-

The pressure of wanting to be accepted is real.

body's parents had a charge account at Dobson's. Finally, one of us decided to be the buyer—I honestly can't remember who it was—but we got an eight-pack of Malt Duck. These were like wine coolers before wine coolers existed. We headed for the patch of woods across the highway from the store and gathered for this momentous occasion. I was anxiety-ridden over how to hide this stunt from my parents; surely they would be able to smell it on my breath, and after fifteen years in my parents' house, I knew they would probably ground me for life. I drank, anyway, and most of us followed our Malt Ducks with our first cigarette, and followed that with our first alcohol-induced vomiting.

To this day, I vividly remember the first sip of that Malt Duck and that first drag of a Benson & Hedges cigarette. I remember throwing up, too, and looking back on that moment—it was like I had found something.

For the rest of high school, I hung out with friends who were a year or two older than me. They were involved in drugs. If I hung with them, they gave me acceptance. As an adult, it is hard to remember just how much a teenager is affected when he or she doesn't make any of the categories in the high school yearbook—categories like best-looking, best-liked, smartest, hardest worker, and most likely to succeed. For those of us who are left out, the rejection is devastating.

That night in the woods across from Dobson's, I had filled a void and never looked back until decades later. You see, at a young age, all of us begin trying to fill a void that only God can fill. We begin worshiping musical artists, athletes, and so forth. God is the only One that deserves our worship, and because I didn't realize this, I set out on a road to destruction.

Temptation

Months passed, and I got used to hiding my smoking and drinking from my parents. One of my friend's parents smoked, so to check if my friend had been smoking, his father smelled his hand. He and the rest of us decided to wear a golf glove while we smoked in case any of our parents had the same idea. There was no end to the things we would do and lies we would tell to continue our mischief. My father said later, "I believed anything you said till you were about fourteen years old." Well, that's about right.

Deception raised its ugly head for me as I walked in our neighborhood one evening. My friend pulled out a joint and offered me some. I had already turned down marijuana many times, thinking to myself that

I would never use illegal drugs. My parents had raised me with a respect for the law. When he saw the hesitation in my face, my friend showed me the rolling papers he had used to make this joint; they were flavored. A flavored rolling paper! That meant the pot would be flavored, right? I don't know. All I know is that the fear I had for pot subsided, and I was ready to give in and try this novelty, this special flavored cigarette.

Not only is addiction harmful, but also it is killing thousands of people. Just like the old cigarette commercials, and just like the beer commercials today that show beautiful people having a wonderful time, this first joint had been dressed up nice. I couldn't see the person addicted to the alcohol, killing themselves and somebody else on the highway. I couldn't see the thousands of broken homes. So it began. I finally said yes to the pot because it was dressed up in flavored paper.

We always need to be on guard, and make right decisions. Those decisions could affect the rest of our lives.

It doesn't matter where you are in your life. If you are a Christian or not, the bible tells us that Satan will come as an *angel of light*. If you are not living for God, the enemy will come at you in the most unexpected of forms; even something so trivial-seeming as flavored rolling paper. If you are a seasoned Christian, the enemy can come at you wearing a choir robe. In other words, we always need to be on guard, and make right decisions. Those decisions could affect the rest of our lives.

Lying

Not long after marijuana took hold of my life, I had to look for a way to continue to smoke pot on my budget. I was a sixteen-year-old in school with a part-time job at a local restaurant, and that salary was not going to support my habit.

The yearning for drugs brings out the addict's creative side. One of my first major lies is one I am not proud of, and it would be followed by hundreds of other lies throughout the years, of which I am not proud, either. I had figured out that if I bought a large amount of pot, I could sell it, make my money back, and have some left over to smoke. I already had some money saved, and I bought the first big load of pot. As long as I could sell it, then everything was okay; as a sixteen-year-old living at home, I was held accountable by my parents for what I did with my money (which, by the way, was the right thing for them to do).

It was a Friday evening in 1978. I was at work and the pot was in my glove compartment, locked up. On a break at work, I went out to my car and realized that my car had been broken into and my pot stolen. I realized that a friend of mine had to be the thief. I was in panic, wondering what I was going to tell my parents about the $125—I'd used it to buy the pot, when it should have been in my wallet. I wracked my brains. All my previous lies were of the "I-didn't-leave-the-mess-on-the-stove" type. This new lie was going to be a big one.

It came to me. I would go home, and the following day, act like my car was broken into at my house and my wallet was taken. That's exactly what I did. The police came and did a report. I went along with all the drama because I had to learn how to bring this lie to a close. Not only did I explain away the cash, but my parents' homeowners insurance reimbursed me for it. They reimbursed me for my pot!

I had gotten through my first bit lie and the fear that came along with it. After that, the lies became easier. To the addicted person, lying becomes a way of life—a necessity, if you will. If you are a family member reading this, don't take the lies personally. Addicts will lie to anyone about anything to get what they want: and that's exactly what I did for the next twenty years.

STRUGGLING WITH ALCOHOL

I was an alcoholic at the age of 16.

Wikipedia refers to alcoholism as compulsive and uncontrolled consumption of alcoholic beverages, usually to the detriment of the drinker's health, personal relationships, and social standing.

According to the 2009 National Statistics on www.dontdrivedrunk.org, we know the following about how a lifestyle geared around drinking can affect others:

All year, 33,808 people were killed in traffic accidents. Exactly 10,839 of these deaths were a result of alcohol (32 percent of all traffic deaths).

An additional 254,000 suffered injuries due to an alcohol related accident.

Drunk drivers kill someone approximately every 48 minutes.

In 2009, 181 children age 14 and younger died in alcohol-related accidents. Over half (92) were riding *with the alcohol-impaired driver*!

Among motorcyclists killed in fatal crashes in 2009, 29 percent had a BAC of over 0.08.

An average drunk driver will drive drunk 87 times before being pulled over.

Drunk driving costs each adult in this country around $500 a year.

One in three people will be involved in an alcohol-related crash in their lifetime.

Among drivers killed in fatal crashes, 30 percent have BACs of 0.08 or greater.

Of the drunk drivers whose licenses are suspended, 75 percent of them continue to drive.

It is legal to buy and is the number-one killer in America. What is a shame is that alcohol is so socially acceptable. Alcohol is what got me started on my road of destruction, and we can say fairly that it is most people's introduction to a lifestyle of addiction.

Addiction and Irresponsibility

At age seventeen I was already drinking heavily on the weekends. It was eleven o'clock one weekend night and I was driving a nice 1978 Cougar, but with just the parking lights on. I was under the influence of Quaaludes, hash, and whiskey—not a good combination.

So here I am, no headlights, driving in front of the police station thinking I am behind a car, which I was indeed. But, it was parked. There was a woman sitting in the parked car waiting for her husband to get off work from his three-to-eleven shift at the ice cream factory across the street. Because of the alcohol and drugs, I really thought her car was moving. I was traveling at about 25 mph when I ran into its back bumper. The impact brought me out of my daze that I was in. Hardly a moment passed and the accident was surrounded by cops.

On that night my car was totaled, I had my first run-in with the police and the court system, and was arrested for a DWI and possession of marijuana.

Worsening matters was the fact that the woman in the car waiting for her husband was pregnant. I don't remember what my thoughts were at that moment but when I sobered up, I prayed, "God please let this unborn child be okay." In the days that followed, my parents and church family were praying for God's protection over this mother and her child, as well. Mercifully, medical checkups confirmed that they had survived my blunder.

†

It was a typical party. This one was about fifty miles from my house—a bad idea from its inception.

At this party, I saw a lot of friends and the draft beer was flowing. When it was time to leave, I fought a battle within myself that I would fight many more times in years to come. *Do I drive, do I stay and sleep it off, or do I have someone drive me home?* It didn't matter if I had arrived at the party having sworn not to drive home; once the alcohol started flowing, I would change my mind. I believed I was invincible, and always ended up driving unless I passed out.

That night, I ended up in a blackout. The struggle was over and the decision was made. *I'm driving home*, I thought. *It's only an hour away.*

I was very familiar with those highways, but somehow, thanks to my blackout, I ended up on a highway that was not going to take me home. From the time I left the party, I cannot recall anything until my truck failed to take the sharp turn on a strange, dark highway. The truck traveled down a forty-five-degree bank until it collided with a con-

> *It is legal to buy the number-one killer in America.*

crete culvert at the bottom. When it came to a halt, my body, face first, was forced into the windshield. At last I emerged from my blackout. My face had gone through the windshield. My nose was broken, blood was everywhere, there was glass in my forehead and face, my chest hurt from the steering wheel, and I had no idea where I was.

All I knew to do was to climb up the bank and peer at the headlights I saw in the distance. The driver stopped and called the ambulance; my parents met us at the hospital. I should have gotten arrested that night but the state trooper at the hospital felt sorry for me and thought I had learned a lesson. He told my family and me that I should have died.

Thank God for His mercy.

†

A few years later, there was another night, another party in Birmingham, and another fifty-mile drive to the safety of my parents' house. When you are drinking, you never think you are as drunk as you are, so you continue to try to perform tasks that you are not capable of performing. This was during a time in my life that I had started selling cars at a new car dealership, and really thought I had found an enjoyable, lucrative job. And one of the perks of that job was driving a new car.

The details that I am about to recount are only the state troopers' suppositions; I had fallen into another alcoholic blackout and cannot remember a thing. As the sun came up that morning, I was driving southbound on a four-lane highway with a large median. What appears to have happened is that I passed out at the wheel with my foot pressing down on the gas pedal, accelerating past all the other vehicles. There was a National Linen truck in front of me traveling at 60 mph, and I approached it doing eighty. I rear-ended the linen truck and began to spin across the median, and headed into the path of northbound traffic. Miraculously, I didn't hit anyone. When my vehicle came to a stop on the shoulder of the highway I was passed out cold, unaware of what had happened.

The first thing I recall after the accident was a state trooper waking me up from what seemed to be an alcoholic coma. Once he got me on my feet and brought me to the police car, I was arrested for a DWI. What was unbelievable was that I left the scene of a totaled vehicle unharmed.

Thank God for His mercy.

✝

Late one night at a party, once again, I had enough to drink that I lost my good judgment. My friend and I were in his panel/cargo van that we used for band equipment; he was the drummer and I was the sound guy. We were good friends. The hour was late and there was a girl that I wanted to see—she did not live far from where we were partying. Once again I had counseled myself that I was okay to drive. I managed to convince my friend to let me drive his van.

As usual, this was a big mistake. Every time I got behind the wheel while drunk, I half-knew what was going on, but when I started driving, the blackout would hit me. That's exactly what happened this night, again.

It was a curvy country road with a steep bank on one side. Apparently I lost control of the van; it rolled down the bank, hit a power pole at the bottom, knocked the power pole down and came to a stop. It's apparent that my body was flung around inside of the cargo van and never once did I wake up. Even when the van came to a stop, I did not wake up. The van was lying on its side and I was lying unconscious, not from an injury but from alcohol.

The power company found me when they responded to the power outage caused by my accident. They finally were able to wake me up and bring me to my senses. What is hard to believe is that the only injury from this wreck was a fractured shoulder.

I got another DWI, and you would think that anybody in their right mind would stop drinking and driving. Alcohol is addicting, however, and I was completely addicted.

✝

It's so hard for people who have never been addicted to look at some of the choices that alcoholics make, and understand why we do the things we do. Well, we don't understand either. Here is one last story.

So, now, here I go again, making another bad choice to drive home after another full night of partying, somehow hoping that the outcome would be different. It was probably seven in the morning and I am on a four-lane highway headed home. There was a light rain falling, making the road a little slick. You can guess what happened next. That's right—another blackout at the wheel. Because of the slick road, as soon as I passed out, the car began to spin out of control. After the first complete turn on the highway, I came to and realized what was happening. As I was waking up, the car did another complete turn, and after two complete turns in the highway I found myself driving in the direction I needed to be going, and I hadn't hit a thing. That was a first.

Almost as soon as I gained control of the car, I saw a convenience store. I turned in to get something to drink and come to my senses. As I was leaving the store and about to get into my car, a man stopped me. He was on his way to go hunting. He was driving a Jeep with a whip

Remember, alcohol is called a spirit, and spirits deceive.

antenna on the back bumper that appeared long enough to raise somebody in Alaska. He called me over to his truck and with his CB in his
hand, and informed me he was behind me while I was doing 360-degree
turns in the middle of the highway. He gave me two options: Either he
was going to call the police to come and arrest me, or I was going to
leave my car there and he would drive me home. Obviously, I chose to be
driven home.

The Deadliest Drug

For centuries, we have referred to alcohol as a spirit. You can ride down
the highway and see a flashing sign that says SPIRITS. We know what
that is: we pull in and buy something to drink, and it will change who
we are.

I attend several college football games each year and I see the
drinking that goes on, especially among students. The universities are
not only producing our next great leaders and educators, but they are
also producing our next generation of alcoholics. Nobody knows if we
are going to drink for the first time and then two years later develop a
drinking problem that we cannot kick. Parents who are not addicted to
alcohol but drink socially in their home are sending the message to their
children that drinking is socially acceptable. If you are a parent, you have
no idea if your child will become an alcoholic or not. You are gambling
with your child's future.

Remember, alcohol is called a *spirit*, and spirits deceive. Alcohol has
deceived people for millennia. It is a trap to believe that just because
someone drinks socially and can stop at any time that all an alcoholic has
to do is just stop. That is not the case.

My entire life, I wanted to drink two beers and be able to stop, but
I never accomplished that. This spirit is deceiving humanity and will
continue to do so. I want to encourage families out there to reject society's messages about alcohol. Your child may be the next person who
can't stop—and it all started with a glass of wine at your dinner table.
Let's stop introducing our children to the number-one most fatal drug
in America.

Alcohol—it is a drug.

STRUGGLING WITH HARD DRUGS

According to the website www.myaddiction.com, statistics show that 10 percent of publicly funded drug abuse center admissions in 2006 were for crack cocaine.

Approximately 36.8 million Americans ages 12 and older had tried cocaine at least once in their lifetimes.

Other statistics show that 19.5 percent of eighth graders, 28.2 percent of tenth graders, and 38.9 percent of twelfth graders surveyed in 2008 reported that powder cocaine was "fairly easy" or "very easy" to obtain (Whitehouse Drug Policy, 2008).

In high school and college, 3.3 percent of students reported being current users of cocaine, meaning that they had used cocaine at least once during the past month.

One out of four Americans between the ages of 26 and 34 has used cocaine in his or her lifetime.

Over 15,000 deaths are annually associated with stimulants in the US (APA).

In 1988, about 300,000 infants were born addicted to cocaine.

The social consequences of heavy cocaine use can be unpleasant. Addicts are likely to eventually alienate family and friends. They tend to become isolated and suspicious. Most of their money and time are spent thinking about how to get more of the drug. The compulsion may become utterly obsessive. The illusion of free will disappears: During a three- to four-day crack binge, users may consume up to fifty rocks a day. To obtain more, crack addicts will often lie, cheat, steal, and commit violent crimes. Once-loved partners and children may be callously cast aside.

I can testify to this personally.

Social Acceptability: The Adult Peer Pressure

I was introduced to cocaine when I was in the automobile business. It was in the 1980s and people in the party scene considered it acceptable. People who had good reputations—successful people—were using cocaine on the weekends.

I heard Bill Cosby say he asked a man one time why he used cocaine, and the man responded, "It intensifies my personality." Mr. Cosby said, "Well, what if you are a jerk?" In the beginning stages of my addiction, cocaine did bring me out of my shell. I was able to communicate with people in a way that I couldn't otherwise. I was more bold and personable. I am in no way condoning going out and using cocaine so you can become more outgoing, but I am telling you honestly, its effect on my behavior was attractive to me in the first month of my addiction. After that, cocaine put me into bondage.

Losing Control of Your Decisions

After being sober for about six months after my first treatment, I was starting to slip back into drinking. I was trying to drink socially. At the time, I was selling cars for a large dealership in Birmingham, Alabama, and really thought I was on a road to success. I drank less often, made money, and had met a woman whom I had grown to love and who loved me. I was able to maintain a car salesman drinking pattern, which meant not getting into any kind of trouble, such as driving while intoxicated, wrecking a car, or getting arrested. You have to understand that alcohol was accepted in the automobile business; actually, being a drinker was almost a requirement.

I didn't realize that I had a God-shaped hole that needed to be filled by God.

I thought deep down inside that she was going to be my final piece of the puzzle. Early in our relationship, however, I knew I was slipping back into my addiction. What I was able to do during a span of about eight months was to just drink alcohol—not that alcohol was the lesser of any evil. She never saw the Gary who was an addict, the Gary who was just waiting to wake up and get back on a road to destruction.

Sobriety was over, and so long as I continued to drink, the drugs were just a matter of time.

As soon as we were married the last threads of self-control broke. The anticipation of actually marrying someone who loved me had been enough to keep me off drugs and avoid the kind of drinking that would scare her off. It sounds really sad, but this is how someone who is longing for acceptance and love thinks—I didn't realize that I had a God-shaped hole that needed to be filled by God. Not very long at all into our marriage I started drinking more heavily, and stayed late at work to drink with the other salesmen. Eventually I could not resist the cocaine. That was the beginning of the end of our marriage.

> It has happened to them according to the true proverb, "A
> DOG RETURNS TO ITS OWN VOMIT," and, "A sow, after
> washing, returns to wallowing in the mire." (2 Peter 2:22)

There was a time shortly after I started snorting cocaine again I went on a three-day binge that would define what I call "the pull and deception of cocaine."

I purchased a large amount of cocaine, and went out of town. I cannot really explain why a husband would leave his wife and just start driving, except *that's the pull and deception of cocaine.*

I can remember two days into this binge of using cocaine. I was in a hotel warring within myself, wanting to stop, afraid to go home, confused, and quite frankly was concerned about my health. Trying to reach out the best way I knew, I called my counselor from rehab and told him my state of mind, what I was doing, and asked him if he could come see me. He couldn't, and asked if I would flush the drugs down the toilet. The problem was that I had been on the phone with him so long that I was starting to crave more cocaine. I told him that I had flushed the drugs, just so I could get off of the phone to continue to use.

That's the pull and deception of cocaine.

The next morning I somehow convinced myself to go home, even though I still had cocaine and was in my third day with no sleep. Continuing to use as I was traveling home, deceiving myself that everything was going to be all right, I concocted the perfect lies to cover my absence for three days.

That's the pull and deception of cocaine.

Not too far from home, I wasn't feeling well. I looked in the rearview mirror to see my face and eyes. My lips were a shade of blue, and I grew really concerned. It was almost immediately I saw an exit for a hospital with an emergency room, so I took the exit. As I was on the exit I took the bag of cocaine and threw it out the window: Only when I was convinced that I might die was I willing to give it up. I checked into the emergency room and told the doctor exactly what I had been doing. He told me my vital signs were in the danger zone. The staff kept me for hours, gave me some medicine to get my vital signs back to normal, and then released me. What happened next was a classic example of how deceptive our hearts can be, especially under the influence of cocaine—I went back to the exit where I had thrown the cocaine out the window, parked my car, and walked up and down the exit searching for it.

That's the pull and deception of cocaine.

I know that this sounds crazy, but the reality is, remorse and guilt are temporary. If you treat your spouse wrong, look at pornography, have an anger problem, or something else of that nature, and you find yourself temporarily getting a handle on these issues for them to only return, it's because the remorse has worn off and you do not have the power to sustain the change. Something divine needs to happen to make the change lifelong.

When It Finally Ruins Your Life

After snorting cocaine for several months while working at the dealership and somehow hiding it from my wife, I took a trip with one of the salesman. It was a road I do not wish on anyone. We went out drinking and snorting cocaine, but he wanted to introduce me to crack cocaine, a smoke-able form that is far more addicting. That was the night that I would enter several years of hell.

The first time I tried crack cocaine, it brought on a one-of-a-kind euphoria that I would never again attain. All I wanted to do was experience that same euphoria, but it never happened. The addiction was so mental that crack cocaine was all I could think about.

I would lie to my wife about places I would go and money that I spent. Because of this new drug, I was disappearing anytime I thought I could think of the right lie. I would try to think of lies that would keep me away from home a couple of days just so I could go to a hotel room and smoke crack cocaine for two or three days at a time. My wife and coworkers knew something bad was going on in my life, but no matter how paranoid I felt, I just didn't care.

I was living the American dream, but no earthly treasures or possessions can change the fact of addiction.

All I wanted was to smoke crack anytime that I could. The drug had such a demonic, mental strangle-hold on my life that if someone had sat me down and told me that if I smoked crack again I would lose my wife, job, and home, and then go to prison, I would somehow work it out in my mind that those consequences would happen to someone else, not me. Crack cocaine addiction makes you feel above the law—invincible, even.

My wife warned me that if I didn't stop she was going to leave me. The final warning came when I arrived home from a three-day binge. I walked into our home and there was a note on the steps that read, *I am gone, it is over.* And it was. Earlier that day I had reached a place in my life where I found myself walking through the projects, after two days without sleep, searching for a dealer in the middle of the day. Now my wife had left me, I was about to lose my job, I was running out of money, and could not stop smoking crack cocaine. If there was any shot at reconciling my marriage after I had started drinking and snorting cocaine again, this new drug quashed it. Without divine intervention, I was beyond help.

I had met a beautiful woman whom I married. I had a beautiful home, an antique convertible, and a good job. I was living the American dream, but no earthly treasures or possessions can change the fact of addiction. The threat of losing it all would not stop me from losing it all. Like my ex-wife told me just before she divorced me, "I do not doubt you love me, but you love something more—the drugs." She was right. The American dream couldn't fix us, and it couldn't fix me. I sunk into a depression whose only antidote was more drugs. And that's exactly what I did for a few more years, moving in and out of jails and rehab. That was my new life.

Prison Time

The pain of divorce fueled my hopeless outlook on life, which fueled my using—the cycle of addiction continued. After many years living like a gypsy, I would end up in Alexandria, Louisiana, but the road to get there was long. I would never stay in an apartment longer than it took for my bad checks to catch up with me, or longer than the eviction process would allow me to stay. I had already spent time selling cars in Atlanta, Tampa, and Birmingham, but could not hold a job for long. The car dealerships would employ me, knowing that I could sell a lot of cars, and would try to sweep my problem under the rug as long as I was making them money. When I was married, the dealership even stopped giving me my check; they would give it to my wife so I would not go out on a binge. They did all they could to save me from myself, and so did the other dealerships.

My last sales job was in Tampa. I had just gotten fired and was about to lose my apartment again—life as normal. I would just go to a home-less mission and find another job or a couch to sleep on. This time I decided to call my uncle in Baton Rouge. He welcomed me, and also got me a job as an electrician's helper. Here we go again, another chance.

After I was asked to leave my uncle's home after my using and stealing became intolerable, I got a job with an electrical company in Alexandria, Louisiana. I went on a binge that would be my last for a while. Living in a hotel, fired for not showing up for work, out of money, and forging checks from a checkbook I had stolen, I was in high gear. Nothing was going to stop me but death or maybe jail.

Thank God it was jail and not death. I spent about three weeks in Alexandria writing bad checks to support my habit and living out of hotels; this was before tele-check. Today I would have never gotten away with this for so long. At a hotel, tired and hopeless, I heard the police came knocking on my door. They were there to arrest me for forgery. I was making an impression around the city, and they were looking for me. They found me, and in some sort of strange way I was happy.

I didn't know how long I was going to be in jail and didn't care. I was tired of the hustle I was living and relieved when the cuffs snapped around my wrists.

I spent a few months in the parish jail before they let me know that I was getting a sentence of two years for forgery, but that I would be able to get out in a year. The time in jail was not easy, but it was actually better than living like I had been. I got my health back and really wanted to live a new life. I went to every chapel service, searching and searching, but I never gave my heart over to God—and as a result, any change that I was searching for was going to be very temporary.

> *I went to every chapel service in jail, but I never gave my heart over to God—and as a result, any change that I was searching for was going to be very temporary.*

You would think that one year in jail totally clean from using drugs and drinking would be enough time to catapult someone into eternal sobriety. It's not. Unless there is a heart change, a life change is not going to happen. I would prove that true soon enough.

✝

My parents had decided to come get me from prison. This gesture was a milestone; they did not trust me with good reason. They came to pick me up and we all had high hopes for my future, but the only thing I had going for me was one year of sobriety. I was still smoking cigarettes, I was proud and arrogant, and though I could see my problems, I just didn't want to admit them. I was home about a month and the cycle started again. I started drinking, which led back to the drugs. I was officially transforming back into the man who had been locked up. I was back, the monster had been awakened, my parents rightfully told me I had to leave, and so the life of a crack addict continued.

Crack cocaine and drinking continued to be a part of my life for at least another five years. I never lived in one place more than a couple of months, was homeless on many occasions, and passed in and out of jails, missions, and programs. This was a very hard life, but I didn't know that I could escape it. The misery became overwhelming. I remember walking the streets, homeless and literally cursing a family under my breath if they looked too happy. Was I mad at them? No, I was mad at myself and envious of any one who was happy—which brings me to an important point.

Who's to Blame?

We tend to blame others for our problems. This is a mistake. There may be cases where others should get the blame for something bad that happened in our life, but no matter what happens, we should never blame God. The consequences addicts face *are not God's fault.* If we blame God, we will never be able to embrace His love and get a grasp of how fully He loves us. Blaming God will never help us on the road to freedom from addiction. If you are a family member of the addicted you will never be free from guilt and will never have a sense of hope for your loved one if you continue to blame God.

I was serving one year of a two-year sentence for forgery in Louisiana. The first month after I was locked up and received my sentence, I had asked God, "Please keep my family safe while I am here." I just didn't know how I could handle something happening to them while I was locked up.

Life's tragedies are a result of living in a world infiltrated with sin, with our will to do whatever we want to do. The results can be painful.

It had probably been a year since I had seen any of my family, so by the time I got out I would have gone over two years without seeing any of them. One month before my release, I got a special phone call. It was to let me know that my brother had been in a car wreck and had slipped into a coma.

I don't ever remember thinking that Randy would die. All I could think about were the many times I should have died and I didn't, so why would God allow Randy to die after being in just one wreck? I think people tell themselves, "It could never happen to me," and that's exactly the way I felt. I assumed that Randy would pull out of this coma and everything would be okay. A few days later I got the phone call that I asked God to protect me from when I started my time in prison Randy had died.

I will never forget the walk back to the cell, the emotions that were racing through me at that time. I think I was hurting more for my parents than anything. They had three sons. Their oldest was in prison and has lived a life of addiction, and the middle son was no longer with us. The pain I felt for my parents was unbearable, and on top of that, I was blaming and questioning God. "Why not me?" I asked. "I'm the one that shouldn't be alive! I have been the bad kid! Why did you take Randy? Especially when that is all I asked is for You to keep my family safe while I am locked up!"

Later in life, none of the tragedies, addictions, failed relationships, or prison sentences was God's fault. All of these things are a result of living in a world infiltrated with sin, with our will to do whatever we want to do. The results can be painful. I was unable to go to my brother's funeral, and the remorse ate at me. I never dealt with it until I trusted God with my life. This lack of trust gave me some hard years—years of being unable to deal with Randy's death because of my anger towards God. I blamed Him for all the bad things that had happened in our lives.

I was eventually able to put my life in His hands, but until that day, the only person that suffered from blaming God was I.

MAKING THE CHANGE

But we had to celebrate and rejoice, for this brother of yours was dead and has begun to live, and was lost and has been found. (Luke 15:32)

I cannot stress enough that prayer brings about change in a person's life. If you know someone who is burdened, continue to pray. Pray they will get to a place—sometimes a hard place—where they will be willing to reach out to something greater, God.

My family, friends, and church family prayed for me often. Because of their prayers, I ended up making the best decision of my life in the summer of 1997. I had been homeless for a while on the west bank of New Orleans, sleeping behind a drug store on Lapalco Boulevard. It was behind that drug store that I slept and drank cheap whiskey until my stomach could no longer hold the alcohol. During the day I would make my way over to the dollar cinema and watch movies all day for one dollar, find an empty large popcorn carton and collect free refills. Once I found one, I could eat popcorn all day and drink water from the water fountain—it was how I survived.

As I walked out of the grocery store one day, carrying stolen cigarettes and beer, I encountered a black man with a collar on. He must have been a minister at the Church of God in Christ, and he had a bunch of kids with him dribbling basketballs and raising money for his church. To this day I can't explain why I walked over to him and asked for prayer. I should have been thinking about getting out of the parking lot before being caught by the police.

Crazy as it sounds, though, that's exactly what I did, and he prayed for me. At that point I don't ever think I had ever felt so hopeless. Maybe this was the beginning of something supernatural, something divine.

Looking back, I know it was. The preacher didn't focus on the beer or cigarettes in my hand. He didn't even mention them, and he didn't say anything about the way I looked. All he did was pray for me.

Later that night in the French Quarter I did what I usually did—drank myself into a blackout. I don't remember exactly what I did, but I got arrested and was sent to Orleans Parish Prison for seven days for public intoxication. Staying in jail for seven days was not a big deal for me. I had already spent about two years of my life behind bars. But this time, something started to happen.

"Look at the Scum in Here!"

> *And whosoever shall exalt himself shall be abased; and he that shall humble himself shall be exalted. (Matthew 23:12)*

We typically think of pride as an affliction of the successful—of someone who drives a nice car and lives in a nice home. But believe it or not, a drug-addicted, jobless, homeless alcoholic in prison can be even prouder than that.

I can remember the anger I had toward the officer processing me into the parish jail, like it was his fault that I was in jail. I was so furious that I was filled with hatred toward the world. I was full of pride and arrogance, and had no hope in sight.

After I was processed, a number of us were placed into a large room to get stripped down and sprayed with something that would kill our parasites. This sounds really gross, I know, but I have to paint the full picture so you can understand how dangerous pride is. As I am writing this, over fourteen years have passed and I remember what happened in that cell like it was yesterday. I

God knew I was ready for a change, even though I didn't know it myself.

looked around; I felt angry at the life I was living and couldn't believe that life had come to this again. You see, I had been locked up many times hoping that the last time *would be the last time.* I was standing in the middle of about twenty men and there was a short, young, nice-looking Hispanic guy next to me. In the middle of my selfish, angry, prideful, and hopeless world I did an inventory of everybody in that cell and then looked down at the Hispanic guy and told him, "Look at the scum in here."

He looked up at me with a confused expression on his face and said, "Dude, you are one of us." Hard to believe that someone in my position would make a statement like that, but that's exactly what pride does to man. It makes you very unattractive to those around you, and God's word says that *He resists the proud.*

Only two days later God would radically change my life—but first, I believe with all my heart He used a Hispanic man in a New Orleans cell to humble me. Who knows; it could have been an angel! A couple of days had passed and I found myself looking for a novel to read, and learned that they were not allowed in Orleans Parish Jail. And then it happened...

Hear the Message

At the very moment that a novel could not be found in jail, the doors opened to our very large dorm. Through the threshold came the Gideons, coming to give a bible to anyone who wanted one. Honestly, if I had a choice between a novel and a bible, I would have chosen the novel. God orchestrated this deal knowing I was ripe and ready for a change, even though I didn't know it myself.

Bored and willing to read anything, I began reading the bible starting with the book of Matthew. I didn't understand everything I read, but I was reading and time was passing—mission accomplished. I continued reading the book of Mark. I started to understand what I was reading, and it was making sense to me. Then there was the book of Luke followed by the book of John. I read this all during the course of one day. At some point while reading the Gospel of John, I started to realize all of these books, all of these accounts of the Gospel, basically said the same thing.

It was then that God started tugging at my heart. I began weeping and right there in that cell I was really sorry for the life I had lived. I told God I was sorry. I told God I wanted a new way of life. I asked for forgiveness, and what happened next was unbelievable.

Conversion

Instantly, the foul language that I always used ceased, and it disturbed me to hear it in the jail cell. I found myself crying a lot over the next couple of days. I had cried in jail before—over losing a job, a marriage, a car, and a home. These tears were different. They were tears of repentance! I was truly sorry for the way I had lived my life, and was ready to move on.

Curled up on my bunk, I cried more tears of repentance. I felt an unprecedented sense of contentment and fulfillment. It really made no sense to me because I was lying in a jail cell with no job, no money, no clothes, and nothing to look forward to beyond my release date.

Something had happened, but I feared the unknowns in my future. There was nothing I could say to any family member or friend that would convince them to allow me back into their lives—I had burned every bridge I had ever crossed. They had heard me profess countless times that I had changed. So, what would I do when I get out? Trust God? That's exactly what I had to do, and some part of me was excited about it; this kind of trust was new to me. I had gotten everything I'd ever had in my life by lying, manipulating, and stealing.

But the experience of trust was still so new that the unknowns gnawed at me. And soon, worry and fear set in…

Don't Worry

> *Therefore I tell you, do not worry about your life.* (*Matthew 6:25*)

God had transformed my life over these last couple of days, but my release date loomed. What was I going to do? Go to a local church and tell them, "I found God. What are you going to do for me?" Well, that sounds foolish, but no other idea sounded any more promising. I was gripped with fear. It was a fear different from any I had ever known, because something supernatural had happened in my life. I knew that I needed to approach life differently; but how was I going to invent a new lifestyle from scratch? The crazy thing is that I had been living on the streets, addicted to drugs and alcohol and didn't worry about anything. Now that I had given my heart to Jesus, all of a sudden, I was anxious.

I couldn't just have faith in myself to survive anymore—I had to have faith in God.

You see, this new life was unfamiliar to me. That is why it is so important to get involved with other Christians and read God's word. (I will talk about this more later in the book.) I worried about where I was going to live, what I was going to eat, where I would work, and so forth. Yet I believe that is exactly what the enemy wants us to do. WORRY.

In His word, God states clearly that he does not want us to worry. Worry is a sin. Jesus says three times in Matthew 6 not to worry. As it turned out, the only way I could pass time in my cell was to read God's word, so that's what I did, and that is where I first understood Matthew 6:

> *Do not worry about what you will eat or drink; or about your body, what you will wear. Is not life more than food, and the body more than clothes? Look at the birds of the air; they do not sow or reap or store away in barns, and yet your heavenly Father feeds them. Are you not much more valuable than they? Can any one of you by worrying add a single hour to your life? (Matthew 6:25–27)*

My worry evaporated. I walked out of that cell a few days later, ready to start my new life, and remembering God's word: "Therefore I tell you do not worry about your life."

Follow the Example Set for You

They let a group of us out of Orleans Parish Prison at 4 a.m. Buses weren't running and neither were the ferries. I really wanted to return to the west bank of New Orleans, which was familiar to me, but that meant taking a ferry across the Mississippi River. When the ferries started running I made my way to the west bank not knowing what I was going to do to survive because I did not want to steal, drink or use drugs anymore. Once I finally made

The change required faith in something greater than me, something which I could not see or touch.

it to the port in Algiers, I was convinced God was going to take care of me. It even sounds crazy now; it definitely sounded crazy then. God was going to take care of me and I actually believed it.

As I walked down a crowded Bell Chase Highway during rush hour, I could not believe what I saw. Immediately the fragile faith I had in God intensified.

It was the preacher that prayed for me!

He was coming out of a store. I approached him and reminded him of how we had met a week ago, and told him what had transpired during my days in jail. I was very excited when I was telling him, and I believe he sincerely shared in that excitement. The one thing most important to me was that I asked him for a bible. I had left my Gideon bible with an inmate who did not have one.

Something supernatural had to be happening in my life, because here was a kindhearted stranger, and in the past I would have immediately tried to manipulate him for my own advantage. Well, *something was different*. As we were talking, I realized there was a woman in the car—his wife. They had an older model station wagon with no air conditioning, in the middle of July in southern Louisiana. Yet the preacher asked me to get in the car. His wife gave me the front seat. This was my first real encounter with a Christian's way of treating a stranger. A homeless stranger—wow! The preacher said, "We are going to the bookstore and purchase you a bible and get you something to eat."

After we had done all that, the preacher started calling people he knew to try to find me a job. He was very regretful in telling me that he didn't have a place for me to stay, and by the way, that was something I hadn't even asked for (out of character for me). *Something was different.* We parted ways that day after not being able to find a job or a place to stay. It was a sad departure, it was the last time I ever saw the preacher, and to this day I still don't know his name.

Peace in the Valley

The last few days had involved situations and events that would change the direction of my life for eternity. The preacher was gone, and it was so tempting to go back to my old ways of stealing and lying to survive on the street. Yet things were different now, and I needed to have faith in what had happened to me in jail: God had touched my heart and I knew it.

I had always kept in touch with my parents, even when times were rough. I hadn't talked to them in a couple of weeks and told myself that I would call home tomorrow. In the meantime, I am questioning the direction of my new life, because really, the only option available was to go back to sleeping behind the K&B drugstore. So, that's exactly what I did. It was a very hot night and a part of me was excited and another part of me was scared because I knew that things needed to be different.

God had captured my heart, but quite honestly it was confusing. The confusion and fear stemmed from the simple fact that the new journey was unknown. It required faith in something greater than me, something which I could not see or touch. The preacher had left me with a few dollars, and I made the bad decision of going into the drugstore and buying some whiskey. It wasn't even like I had warred within myself whether to drink or not—it was habit, and I just did it.

Well what about the change? Foul language was now hard for me to hear, cigarette smoke was a stench to my nostrils, and I was making the decision to drink? I can't explain it other than as a symptom of my human fallibility: Who gets everything right the moment they give their hearts to God?

As the years continue to pass and I reflect upon that night, I continue to get a new appreciation of the Grace of God. After I had gotten drunk for the last time, I was sitting on a bench in front of the drug store late that night, and started to weep about what seemed to be a hopeless situation. I really didn't see a way out even though I wanted out badly. I just wanted a normal life. Then out of nowhere, a memory of a childhood church hymn returned to me. I started singing "Peace in the Valley."

Well I'm so tired and so weary
But I must go alone
Till the lord comes and calls
Calls me away, oh yeah.
Well the morning's so bright
And the lamp is a light,
And the night, night is as black as the sea,
And there will be peace in the valley for me someday.
There will be peace in the valley for me, oh Lord I pray

There'll be no sadness, no sorrow, no trouble I see.
There will be peace in the valley for me.

As I look back on that night, knowing the preacher prayed for me, and that my family, church, and friends had been praying for me, I realized I was praying for myself.

Well, I'm so tired and so weary.
There will be peace in the valley for me, oh Lord I pray
There'll be no sadness, no sorrow, no trouble I see.
There will be peace in the valley for me.

And little did I know…

FAMILIES, THERE IS HOPE

LESSONS FROM THE PRODIGAL SON

In the last days of my addiction, before my conversion, there is a time that I think about often which still breaks my heart. It's just one example of what a drug addict will do and say to the ones they love. They will do and say anything—and families, you cannot take it personally. It is the addiction talking, and not your family member or friend.

It was one of those times when I had been on a cocaine binge living from crack house to crack house. I was dealing with an emotion that I had faced many times: the hopeless feeling you get when you are out of drugs and money, and have no job and no place to live. It is an empty feeling, a feeling that will consume and take control of you if you let it. You will do things that you would never think about in a sober frame of mind. That is one of the terrible things about crack cocaine. Cocaine takes you to such euphoric places that the crash is almost unbearable; you feel so bad that your only thought is of how to use again.

After one of these crashes, and feeling very depressed and desperate, I was wondering whom to call. Who might believe a sob story and send me money? I had already burned the bridge with my parents, and pretty much everybody else I knew. I decided to call my grandmother. I started my crying routine, lying, *Families, you cannot take it personally.* saying if I didn't get any money for food and shelter, I was going to kill myself. I didn't care if my call caused her to worry about me—I only cared about money, which she was wise enough not to give me.

You have to understand that a desperate drug addict will say anything to manipulate your emotions. If they feel it's necessary to say, "I hate you," in order to get what they want, they will say it.

You can't take it personally. They will blame you for their problem, they will blame circumstances—in fact, they will shift the blame to anything or anybody but themselves. It is the voice of addiction speaking, and not the person you love.

The Conundrum

You may ask yourself how your loved one managed to travel so far down the road of addiction that they lose their voice to it. You will certainly wonder how you can help without contributing to his or her problem. The kind of support you offer will make a difference, if you offer it understanding the examples God's word has given you, and look to it for guidance. Some Christians expect that the Lord is the kind of parent who protects them from all sorrow and disappointment. But that's not the kind of Father He is. He lovingly allows His children to experience suffering. If you are a parent, what kind are you? Do you try too hard to make your kids happy? And is your effort having the opposite effect? These questions introduce an interview with Lori Gottlieb, author of an article on the subject of unhappy young adults (*The Atlantic*, July–August 2011 issue). Her conclusion: Yes. Parents who refuse to let their children experience failure or sadness give them a false worldview that does not prepare them for the harsh realities of adult life. The children are left feeling empty and anxious.

I can remember being homeless on the streets in Birmingham, only fifty miles from my parents' middleclass home. They did not come to rescue me. They may not admit it now, but I know that deep down they felt that if I didn't learn the consequences of my actions, and if my family got in the way of me experiencing those consequences, I would never learn from my mistakes. They had already protected me from experiencing consequences early in my life, and I am sure they wish they had stepped back earlier. But they had learned their lesson, and they absolutely did the right thing by allowing me to experience the streets.

God gives us the same example: In Luke 15, Jesus tells the story of the prodigal son. I will use this story to frame the rest of this chapter, and interpret its lessons in the context of addiction. But let's sum it up here, first. A man has two sons. The younger son asks his father to give him his portion of the family estate as an early inheritance. Once received, the son sets off on a long

Pray, think long and deeply, and communicate with spouses to make the best possible decisions for our children.

journey to a distant land and begins to waste his fortune on wild living. When the money runs out, a severe famine hits the country and the son finds himself in dire circumstances. He takes a job feeding pigs. He is so destitute that he even longs to eat the food assigned to the pigs.

The young man finally comes to his senses, remembering his father. In humility, he recognizes his foolishness, decides to return to his father and ask for forgiveness and mercy. The father, who had been watching and waiting, receives his son back with open arms of compassion. He is overjoyed by the return of his lost son. Immediately the father turns to his servants and asks them to prepare a giant feast in celebration.

Meanwhile, the older son is not one bit happy when he comes in from working the fields and discovers a party going on to celebrate his younger brother's return. The father tries to dissuade the older brother from his jealous rage, explaining, "You are always with me, and everything I have is yours—but your brother who was dead has begun to live."

Two Sons

> And He said, "A man had two sons. The younger of them said
> to his father, 'Father, give me the share of the estate that falls to
> me.' So he divided his wealth between them. (Luke 15:11–12)

Our family had three sons that all made some bad choices. I was the one who made a million and lived like the prodigal in a distant land. Every family in the world is going to have children who make some bad decisions, decisions that parents probably made growing up that we don't want to see repeated in our children.

Many households in America have more than one child, and each one is different. They will live differently; they will have different personalities; and they will definitely create situations that require you to make hard decisions. You will probably not be able to make the same choices for one child as you would make for the other, and because of this, you may think that you are not being fair.

Don't allow yourself to feel that way. Fear of unfairness to one of your children keeps parents from making right decisions—decisions appropriate for each individual situation. What we need to do when we find ourselves having to make decisions on behalf of our children is to pray, think long and deeply, and communicate with spouses to make the best possible decisions for our children. They are worth it.

Remember, too, that discipline is work! I see many people coming to Teen Challenge who were raised by lazy parents, parents afraid of proper disciple and unwilling to pray and think deeply about what is right for their children. This laziness doesn't mean they don't love their children, but the work of discipline is hard, and God expects parents to make the effort.

One Was Bad

> *And not many days later, the younger son gathered everything together and went on a journey into a distant country, and there he squandered his estate with loose living. (Luke 15:13)*

How many times do parents, meaning well, give their children wonderful gifts prematurely, only to find out that the children were not mature enough to handle the gifts? In these cases, we have done them more harm than good. It's like an eighteen-year-old going to the NBA—now he's an instant millionaire and has a lot of issues related to the gap between the level of his wealth and the level of his maturity. The only thing that sometimes keeps them out of trouble is the money that is getting them in trouble.

I knew a couple that gave their grandchild a large sum of money as an early high school graduation gift. This was two months before he graduated. After he received the money, he dropped out of high school, moved to the beach, and squandered it. That boy is no longer alive today as a result of his addiction. I am not saying that the grandparents are wholly to blame for what happened to their grandchild, but we need to use wisdom and allow our children to earn what they have.

I cringe when someone graduates from our program, and their parents immediately buy them a car, get them a cell phone, and give them money. Please, let them work their way back, and obtain the things they need in this world with the work of their hands. Instead of taking care of or enabling an adult child, allow them to accomplish something they can be proud of.

Allow Them to Work!

> *So he went and hired himself out to one of the citizens of that country, and he sent him into his fields to feed swine.* (*Luke 15:15*)

After the younger son had spent everything he had on a lifestyle of sin, the bible tells us that he got a menial job. His job was to feed pigs in a field.

I was that young man in a pigpen. I am grateful today for the times that my parents refused to come bring me home—I believe that is one of the reasons I am alive today. When I read this parable, I believe that the father knew where his son was—this was before planes, trains, and automobiles, so his son couldn't have traveled far. The fact is, though, the father did not come to his son's rescue. The son was allowed to experience the pain and consequences of losing everything. He was allowed to work a job that most parents today would consider a sign of failure. We don't want our neighbors to find out our child is working in a pigpen, so we step in and find something else for them when God really wanted to teach them something in that pigpen. Of course we don't want our children working at a burger joint, but sometimes, if they have squandered away other opportunities, it is worse to protect them from that job—it may be a life lesson that God wants to teach our children. Don't let your social pride tempt you to protect them from God's teaching hand.

I often see families enable their children to continue doing the same things over and over again. God is merciful and gracious, but sometimes He wants us to let go and allow our children, His children, to experience life-changing consequences. It's not easy, especially if your child gets arrested and they cry

Don't protect your children from God's teaching hand.

and say hurtful things toward you because you will not bail them out jail. But we need to understand that God is perfect and we as parents do not have the ability to be perfect. Knowing that God is perfect, we need to let go and allow God to be the one who chooses between mercy and discipline.

We tend to want to be merciful when actually we are creating an atmosphere of disbelief. Our children don't believe us. For example, if we give our teenager a curfew, and threaten him with grounding if he comes home late, we cannot be merciful with the consequences. If he comes home after his 10 p.m. curfew and we do not ground him, we have just sent him the message that we are not serious about what we said—we basically lied to them. What we are doing is laying the groundwork for them to always doubt our word.

Let Them Wallow

> *And he would have gladly filled his stomach with*
> *the pods that the swine were eating and no one*
> *was giving anything to him. (Luke 15:16)*

The bible tells us that after he was working in the field feeding pigs, he would have been glad to be able to eat what the pigs were eating. Pigs were unclean animals. Jews were not even allowed to touch pigs. When the son took a job feeding pigs, even longing for their food to fill his belly, it reveals that he had fallen as low as he could possibly go. This son represents a person living in rebellion to God. Sometimes we have to hit rock bottom before we come to our senses and recognize our sin.

There were many times in my life that my parents could have rescued me from being homeless on the streets, but they didn't. Parents need to realize that the obituaries are not full of people that died of starvation in the United States of America. People who are without means can always find something to eat, and even shelter for the night at homeless missions all around the country. They may not find what they *want* to eat, but there is always a meal available in America. Do not fear of someone you love starving on the streets; we need to allow them to wallow so that they will have an opportunity to come to their senses.

I cannot even begin to count the times that I have seen adults as old as forty years old go through a trial while they are in our program. They may not be able to get along with their roommate or a staff member, or may have gotten some type of discipline for a rule they broke. They will call their mom or dad, and that parent will come pick their forty-year-old child up from our program to essentially protect them from God's teaching hand. That is classic enabling and codependency behavior. Some loved ones are themselves addicted to drama, addicted to having to help someone, addicted to being depended upon. Avoid this trap of codependency! Let your loved one experience the pain that will bring about change. Let them wallow so they can get better.

Know When They Have Come to Their Senses

> *But when he came to his senses... (Luke 15:17)*

Recognizing when someone has come to his or her senses can sometimes be difficult. We need to rely on our knowledge of that person. If it's your child or close family member, you obviously know him or her very well—trust in that knowledge.

A good sign that the prodigal child had come to his senses is found in Luke 15:18–19. He says, "I will get up and go to my father, and will say to him, 'Father, I have sinned against heaven, and in your sight; I am no longer worthy to be called your son; make me as one of your hired men.'" The son recognized that he had sinned against his father by not honoring him. He showed humility by saying he was unworthy to be called a son; he was not saying this to condemn his father's parenting. Then he told his dad, "I just want to be like one of your hired men. Consider hiring me."

He didn't come home and ask for his allowance back, his old room back, or his car keys. I can recall spending a year in prison, and wanting better living conditions. My parents had said that they were going to bring me home and give me another chance. When they told me this, I didn't thank them—I started making demands about my accommodations. What a terrible case of pride! And that pride led me to another fall. I had not come to my senses. Here are some signs of pride that will help you determine whether a person has come to their senses, or if they are still enslaved by pride:

Are their feelings hurt easily?

Does it irritate them when people don't agree with them?

Does it really bother them when someone corrects their mistakes?

Is it hard for them to admit mistakes?

Do they think they are usually right and others are usually wrong?

Do they find it hard to compromise? Is it their way or no way?

Are they often stressed?

Do they find themselves giving more criticism than compliments?

Are they quick to judge other people on first appearances?

Are they usually more concerned with their own needs and wants than the needs of people they are with?

If someone has hurt them or done them wrong in the past, do they hold bitterness and resentment against that person?

Do they seek praise for things over which they have no control (e.g., beauty, talents, abilities)?

Do they feel offended or unappreciated when not given credit for something they have done?

Do they often compete or compare themselves with someone else?

Are they always trying to do better or have more than some other particular person?

Do they neglect seeking the help of God in Scripture and prayer, and neglect seeking the help of others in the Christian community?

Do they see themselves as having eliminated most of the sin in their lives or as having very little sin?

When I was in Teen Challenge I recognized that I had come to my senses when I would talk to my mom on the phone and she would ask me did I need any money? I would have no money, but I had everything I needed—toiletries, classroom materials, and clothing. So I could not tell her I needed money so that I could spend it on ice cream. Ice cream was not something I needed. I had come to my senses.

Celebrate Their Return

> *So he got up and came to his father. But while he was still a long way off, his father saw him and felt compassion for him, and ran and embraced him and kissed him. (Luke 15:20)*

The father is a picture of the Heavenly Father. God waits patiently, with loving compassion, to restore us when we return to him with humble hearts. He offers us everything in his kingdom, restoring the full relationship with joyful celebration. He doesn't even dwell on our past waywardness.

If we have a wayward loved one who has squandered their life but has repented and come to their senses, then we need to show God's grace and forgiveness. It doesn't mean that we trust them immediately—trust and forgiveness are totally different. We need to *celebrate* their return; not to say, "I told you so. I wish you had listened to me," and so forth. This is not the time.

I do not encourage giving money as part of the celebration, nor purchasing a cell phone, nor buying a car. They need to earn these things to gain an appreciation for them, without stirring up an easier sense of entitlement. It's simply time to welcome the prodigal loved one home with open arms full of grace and forgiveness.

Are all these suggestions a guarantee? No—people still have a free will. But we can look to Jesus' parable of the prodigal son and his father to help us make the best decisions we can. We can pray and believe, too; but remember, prayer and faith without action do not get us anywhere. We need to believe and pray that God will deliver people from addictions, but we do our part as well. As it is written in James 2:20, "Faith without works is useless."

Don't Be Self-righteous with an Addict

An addict is someone whose sin is publically manifested. We all have sin in our life. Someone may be addicted to pornography and no one will ever find out about it, but we tend to look down on the drug and alcohol addict's sin because society has trained us to do so. Release any self-righteous, hypocritical attitude toward the addict. We all have our struggles. We do not need to be like the prodigal son's older brother, who did not want to celebrate the coming home of his lost sibling.

> *Now his older son was in the field, and when he came and approached the house, he heard music and dancing. And he summoned one of the servants and began inquiring what these things could be. And he said to him, "Your brother has come, and your father has killed the fatted calf because he has received him back safe and sound." But he became angry and was not willing to go in; and his father came out and began pleading with him. But he answered and said to his father, "Look! For so many years I have been serving you and I have never neglected a command of yours; and yet you have never given me a young goat, so that I might celebrate with my friends; but when this son of yours came, who has devoured your wealth with prostitutes, you killed the fatted calf for him." And he said to him, "Son, you have always been with me, and all that is mine is yours. But we had to celebrate and rejoice, for this brother of yours was dead and has begun to live, and was lost and has been found." (Luke 15:25–32)*

Reading from the beginning of Chapter 15, we see that the older son is a picture of the Pharisees, who in their self-righteousness, have forgotten to rejoice when a sinner returns to God. Bitterness and resentment keeps the older son from forgiving his younger brother.

Questions for Reflection

Who are you in this story? Are you the father, preparing the fatted calf because his son has repented? Are you the rebellious son, lost and far from God? Are you the self-righteous Pharisee, no longer capable of rejoicing when a sinner returns to God? Maybe you've hit rock bottom, come to your senses and decided to run to God's open arms of compassion and mercy? Or are you one of the servants in the household, rejoicing with the father when a lost son finds his way home?

From Aunt Barb

Gary delivered the eulogy this past February at his granny's funeral—the same grandmother whom he loved with all his heart, and whom he had deceived and robbed during his years of addiction. He began her tribute with a statement that mesmerized me. Without an ounce of pretense, he stood in front of his parents, family, and friends and stated that out of all of his grandmothers' grandchildren, *he* was the least likely, or deserving, to be standing before them giving her eulogy.

As I see it, he couldn't have been more wrong. His granny believed with every fiber of her being that a life lived for Jesus, and that the power of a persons' belief in Jesus, the belief that Jesus died for our sins, and that all who believe in him will have everlasting life, can, and *will* conquer anything.

I had the privilege of reading this manuscript before it was edited and published. What resonates from these pages is his unwavering desire to ignite the passion for Christ in those in need, and that a Christ-centered life is the only way out of the depths of addiction. As I finished this manuscript, it confirmed to me

With God at the helm, all things are possible.

that Gary's story is living proof of his granny's unwavering belief, and a testimony to her and his life, that with God at the helm, *all* things are possible. There was no other person God would have wanted standing there at the front of the church on that sad day.

From Mom

Many times I have often thought about the fact that our first son was the guinea pig. Why him? Because he was the first of three sons and living in a fast world of working parents, one of them a swing shifter. We would write notes to one another, and the boys would sign No. 1, 2 or 3 rather than their names. I was only 19 when Gary—No. 1—was born. I did not read Dr. Spock, the guru of the day. I followed my heart, what I thought my parents, my church family, or a wonderful pediatrician would do. I look back and know mistakes were made in his basic upbringing, but I also know he was always loved.

To me, Gary was a model son until around fifteen or sixteen. To be honest, I did not have any idea what changed at the time. You see, I considered myself a very naïve mom, and once again, No. 1 was the guinea pig. Everything I did was connected with family or church, and I really knew nothing else about what was going on with the teenagers of that day. I just felt I had a wonderful family and was very happy.

Gary began to noticeably change. The change I remember the most was that he did not march with the band at a football game. Anything he had done was with a passion, and he was an excellent saxophone player. When he refused to march, I knew something was going on. This was the beginning of a long road.

Fast-forward approximately seventeen years to a Wednesday night—a night when a mom and dad's hearts were breaking because we knew something major was wrong in the life of our eldest son. I thank God for a church family that worshiped on Wednesday night. Life is about choices. My choice was to go to church on that Wednesday night rather than stay home and think what I have done wrong. Praise God, from whom all blessings flow!

> *My prayer for you is to not blame yourself or God, but to turn to God completely.*

God had this all worked out, and I did not have a clue. I know I was supposed to be in His house that night so that He could take care of it all. And He did. I shared with the interim pastor the many concerns about our son; he knew about Teen Challenge, and shared its story with me. I had never heard of Teen Challenge, but God's timing is perfect, and all the right people were in place to transform my son's life. God showed up and showed out.

I think about the seventeen bad years and whose fault they are. I do know one thing for sure. They most definitely were not God's fault, and I do not think they were our fault. They were the result of bad choices, very bad choices, by our No. 1 son. The most recent, excellent fourteen years have indeed been God's fault. He not only changed our No. 1 son's life but He changed our family forever.

This mom is a blessed, thankful mom. I have never, never blamed God or myself. My prayer for those of you who may be reading this is to not blame yourself or God, but to turn to God completely. Give Him everything and He will once again show up and show out. You will never have a complete family if you do not have God.

From Matt

Because of an age difference of ten years, I really never got to know my brother, Gary. When Randy, our middle brother, would pick at me in a "brotherly love" kind of way, I remember Gary defending me. Then it seemed like Gary wasn't around much.

Our house was a loving home, but you knew something was wrong. Things just weren't "the Cleavers." Looking back, I see three boys with something missing. What was missing was not a loving home or caring parents. We had that. We were in a constant search for anything of the world to fill the empty hole we felt in ourselves. We were brought up in church, we were taught how to act, and we acted very well. We were polite kids, and we spent a lot of time together until we started searching.

Gary, being the oldest, began his search first. Randy followed closely behind. Later, I came into the searching club. By this time, Gary was gone—he had disconnected. Randy and I hung out a little, but I spent a lot of time seeking the plug for the hole I was trying to fill. I had learned from Gary and Randy's mistakes how far I could push the envelope and not get caught.

When we lost Randy, I was in disbelief. I didn't realize how someone so young could literally be by your side in one second and gone in the next second. At this time, Gary was in jail and we had no relationship. I was angry with him for not being there. I sought out Randy's friends as a temporary plug.

Fast-forwarding. Gary went to Teen Challenge for help. Teen Challenge didn't fill the hole, but what they taught did. It changed Gary in a way that was not conceivable by the world. It was a night and day change. I, on the other hand, was living a double life. One was churchlike and the other was Matt-like. My hole was still there. Gary had filled his with this thing called Christ. I had heard about Christ all my life (much like Gary) and read about his miracles and probably witnessed a few, but wasn't affected until I saw the night-and-day change in Gary.

Don't get me wrong, I was no different from him, and was a little mad about and jealous of his change. I guess what I'm trying to say is that, for whatever reason, God filled our holes with the only thing that could fill them, and that was with Himself. He used the awesome example in Gary's life to change me. It helped me become more like Christ. God used Teen Challenge to fill Gary's God-size hole, and also filled mine. I love my brother for not quitting, for seeking God's will, and especially for not giving up on me.

We were born brothers, became estranged, and had to become brothers in Christ before we could become blood brothers again. What a testimony!

He is truly an *awesome God*.

ARE YOU OFFERING SUPPORT, OR ENABLING?

One day, my father said, "Son, I am going to make sure that I am not responsible for your death." Now what he meant by that was, *It is not my money or my help that will enable you to make a choice that could cost you your life.* It was the best decision he ever made as a father of someone struggling with addiction.

Are You an Enabler?

An enabler is a person who, acting out of a sincere sense of love, loyalty, and concern, steps in to protect, cover up, make excuses, and become responsible for the chemically dependent person. This can prevent the addict from reaching the crisis that might bring about change, and thereby prolonging his or her illness. Some common enabling behaviors, taken from the helpful website www.drphil.com, are as follows:

Avoiding problems by trying to keep the peace. Believing that a lack of conflict will solve problems.

Denying that the person is using drugs or is chemically dependent.

Keeping your feelings inside.

Minimizing: "It's not so bad. Things will get better when…"

Lecturing, blaming, or criticizing the chemically dependent person.

Taking over his or her responsibilities.

Protecting the chemically dependent person from pain.

Feeling superior; treating the dependent person like a child.

Trying to control the dependent person.

People often wonder if certain steps they are taking would be considered enabling. If you have an adult child who has an apartment, and you pay their electricity bill and rent, and buy food for their refrigerator, you are enabling. Even though you do not give them cash, which they would take and buy drugs with, you have enabled them to use their money to buy drugs instead of using it on rent, lights, food, and gasoline.

In Luke 15:11–32, we read a story of a father letting his son hit bottom because of his foolish behavior. Eventually the son comes home and the father rejoices, but the bible is very clear that the father did not rescue his son. Also, it is interesting that the bible tells us that the son had "come to his senses" and also returned home humbled. He returned asking to be like one of his father's servants. If you have a family member you feel you are enabling, ask God to give you the wisdom and grace to do what's right for him or her.

IMAGES

Mom, Dad, and Gary.

Gary, two years old.

Gary, three years old.

Gary (top); Mom, Dad, and Matt (bottom left); Randy (bottom right).

Left to right: Randy, Matt, and Gary.

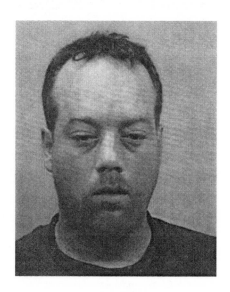

Gary's mug shot, 1996.

Teen Challenge graduation, 1998. Left to right: Granny, Gary, Dad, and Mom.

Teen Challenge Graduation, Mom and Gary.

Gary and Sandy on their wedding day, 1999.

Gary's family. Left to right: Sandy, granddaughter Savanna, Gary, daughter Krysti, granddaughter Mercedes, and son-in-law Glenn.

New Orleans ribbon cutting ceremony after post–Katrina restoration, which repaired damage from seven feet of water. Left to right: Former Teen Challenge USA president Mike Hodges and wife Betty; founders and CEOs of Louisiana Teen Challenge, Greg and Gail Dill; COO of Louisiana Teen Challenge, Gary and Sandy Bentley. Louisiana Teen Challenge is presently operating six residential facilities which houses over one hundred men, women and their families.

TEEN CHALLENGE

GOD HAD MOM ON IT

While all these events were taking place in my life over the past few days—praying with the preacher, getting arrested, meeting God, seeing the preacher again, and drinking for the last time—God, the Master Chess Player, knew what I needed. He was dealing with my mom back in Alabama. God had led my mom to ask her interim pastor if he knew of any place that could help her son. We hadn't talked; she just felt things weren't good and she was right—well, God was right!

Now, my mom and dad had lost all faith in any facility that said it was going to help their son get clean. Because God was in the process of working a miracle, though, my mom reached out to her interim pastor, who didn't know too much about my situation. What is even more miraculous is that the pastor who had recently left the church didn't have the information that my mom was about to receive from her interim pastor.

Mom shared a little of my history and confessed that she felt things weren't well with me. When she talked with me again she wanted to offer me some help. She also explained that all my secular rehab attempts over the years had failed. She wanted to know if there was a Christian program that would help her son. The interim pastor gave my mom the numbers to two Christian programs, one in Mississippi and one in New Orleans. The one in Mississippi was six months, and the one in New Orleans was one year. Both were Christian programs that relied on a relationship with Jesus Christ to facilitate change in an individual's life.

The very next day I made a phone call to my mom, not knowing that she had talked to her interim pastor. She didn't know what had transpired in my life over the last few days—but God knew, and was once again moving some chess pieces. After we had talked for a few minutes, mom said almost apologetically, "Gary, I hope you don't mind, but I have felt that things are not well with you and I know you don't want to go to another 'program,' so I have talked to a pastor who is filling in at our church, and he gave me some phone numbers, and Gary, these are Christian programs. Will you give one a try?"

I was so excited and told her I would love to. I shared with her what had happened over the past week and she told me, "Gary, this feels right." I said, "Yes, it does—I'm excited!" I just knew that God had heard our cry. The very next day I walked fifteen miles to enter Greater New Orleans Teen Challenge.

A yearlong program should have not been my first choice. Let's face it. Who would want to go somewhere for a year when a program offering the same result in six months is available? It doesn't take a genius to figure that one out. But there was one thing that was clear: I needed to stop making decisions based on what I thought was right, because what I thought was right has caused me heartache and pain for seventeen years.

So how did I choose the yearlong program? A few days earlier while

I was already excited about this new life. I just didn't know how I was going to walk it.

I was in jail, I was watching television in the cafeteria at dinner. I saw a ninety second clip on Teen Challenge, a program that had just started taking residents into their program; it just so happened that program was the yearlong program. When my mom said "Teen Challenge" on the phone, I immediately recalled that news clip, and knew that's just where God wanted me to be.

A Brief History of the Program

Teen Challenge was started in Brooklyn, New York in 1958 by Reverend David Wilkerson.

Wilkerson was a young country preacher pastoring a church in eastern Pennsylvania. One February afternoon, Wilkerson read an article in *LIFE* magazine about seven teenagers who were on trial for murder. During a gang fight in Manhattan, these teens had beaten a young man to death. Troubled by what he read in the article, and sensing God wanted him to do something for the teens, Wilkerson made a trip from his hometown of Philipsburg, Pennsylvania to New York City.

Sometime after this, Rev. Wilkerson resigned his church in Pennsylvania and moved to the New York City area to work full-time with teenage gang members. This new work was eventually called "Teen Challenge." Soon, Teen Challenge began to also offer help to those addicted to drugs and alcohol.

During these early years, the organization operated out of a large home on Clinton Avenue in Brooklyn, and from it, ran yearlong residential discipleship programs. The Teen Challenge program is still helping people change their lives today. Due to its success, residential Teen Challenge centers began to spread to cities all across America.

Most of the centers offer a twelve- to eighteen-month residential program for men, women, boys, or girls. These centers are designed to help individuals learn how to live drug-free lives. The programs are discipline-oriented and offer a balance of Bible classes, work assignments, and recreation.

As of 2012, at the beginning of its fifty-second year, there were two hundred Teen Challenge programs in the United States and about three hundred in other countries around the world. A study completed by NIDA in 1974 claimed an 86 percent success rate seven years after graduation. Other studies have been completed since that time which confirmed those findings.

The rest of the story of Teen Challenge is told in the best-selling book, *The Cross and the Switchblade*. This book has sold tens of millions of copies and has been translated into thirty-five different languages. Another exciting book that is available, *Run Baby Run*, tells of notorious gang member Nicky Cruz who was one of David Wilkerson's early converts in New York City. Beyond the *Cross and the Switchblade*, *The Cross Is Still Mightier than the Switchblade* also details Teen Challenge's important early history.

Today, Teen Challenge has grown into one of the largest and most successful programs of its kind in the world.

Teen Challenge Mission Statement

> *To provide youth, adults, and families with an effective and*
> *comprehensive Christian faith-based solution to life-controlling*
> *drug and alcohol problems in order to become productive members*

*of society. By applying biblical principles, Teen Challenge endeavors
to help people become mentally sound, emotionally balanced, socially
adjusted, physically well, and spiritually alive. Through committed
staff and effective programs, Teen Challenge seeks to produce graduates
who function responsibly and productively in society, and who have
healthy relationships in the workplace, family, church, and community.*

Walking Through the Doors

That day is forever etched in my mind: a fifteen-mile walk to get to
Greater New Orleans Teen Challenge, on a very hot July day in 1997.
God obviously knew what had transpired in my life over the past few
days. Shortly after He touched my heart, I was drunkenly singing "Peace
in the Valley." I really believe that was a cry and prayer from the depths
of my soul. The result is God knew I needed this one-year program so I
could learn how to walk with Him and get a foundation in His principles so I would never have to worry about addiction ever again.

God had already saved me before I came into the program, which
is not the case for most of the men and women that come into Teen
Challenge. I was already excited about this new life. I just didn't know
how I was going to walk it. That's exactly what I learned over the next
year in Teen Challenge, the best year of my life!

Teen Challenge basically gave me all the biblical tools, love, and discipline I needed to continue with my new life. I spent the first four months
of the program at Greater New Orleans Teen Challenge, receiving the
foundation that is vital in a new believer's life. After the four months in
New Orleans, I was sent to a second-phase program in Rehrersburgh,
Pennsylvania for eight months. This place was nicknamed The Farm
and was situated on three hundred acres. There were dormitories and
classrooms, a chapel, and various areas of light industry that the students
worked to bring in money to support the program.

Teen Challenge didn't cost me any money, and I was grateful to be
able to earn my way through this life-saving program. I learned so much
about myself while I was there. Through prayer, awesome preaching, and
great classes, I was literally transformed by God's word. Graduation
from the program was not going to be the cure-all for me, but it gave me

the biblical foundation and tools I needed to continue on my own and live a successful life for Christ.

THE CALL—MORE THAN AN EMOTIONAL EXPERIENCE

Behold, you will call a nation you do not know, and a nation which knows you not will run to you, because of the Lord your God, even the Holy One of Israel; for He has glorified you. (Isaiah 55:5)

During my time in Teen Challenge, I learned to really enjoy the new life that I had found in serving Christ. It's like my senses were awakened—a new life began, and I loved it.

It was one thing to be clean for several months, which was familiar to me. I had been clean for one year in prison, but I wasn't free from drugs and was not born again. The born-again experience was literally like the old Gary had died and an unfamiliar new one was alive. I was like a baby learning how to crawl, walk, and talk. I was a new creation.

Even so, it was about eight months into the program and I was starting to get a little uneasy about my future. God was getting ready to change that, as well. All I ever knew was finding work, probably selling cars, making money, and life going on. But every time I would think about a scenario like this, I would be anxious—I couldn't understand what I was supposed to do when I completed Teen Challenge.

One night I went to the chapel, which was open for us anytime. That night I was really seeking God for peace, not necessarily direction. After some time in the chapel, I felt so close to God that I felt Him call me to the ministry almost the way Uncle Sam would call someone into the armed forces. It was just like that. He didn't tell me what I was

There is peace in just saying yes, I'm yours.

supposed to do in ministry, or even what direction I should go. The most likely options, though, were bible school or Teen Challenge. That night, I felt nothing but a strong, vague desire. The peace that overwhelmed me was akin to the peace of God first coming into my life when I accepted Him as my Savior. I said yes; I didn't need to know what I was going to do. There was enough peace in just saying yes, I'm yours. I said no to all self-sufficiency that night and I was happy as a result of answering the call.

†

Close to completing Teen Challenge, many opportunities came my way. I was looking into bible school, considering staying on with Teen Challenge in Pennsylvania, and also going back to New Orleans Teen Challenge.

I had one other wish, too. I was in a traveling choir that went around to different churches sharing what God had done in our life through songs and testimonies. One day we visited a chapel service at a bible college in Valley Forge, Pennsylvania, and sang a couple of songs. I looked out over the crowd and saw all the beautiful Christian women worshipping God—and felt certain that I wanted to get married again. I wanted to marry someone who would be okay with my being in ministry.

It was not many days after this chapel service that my excitement for bible school continued to grow. Another night alone in the chapel, weeks away from graduation, I was now praying for direction. I asked God, "What bible school should I choose?"

It was not long after I started asking God for direction that He told me that I was going to bible school to find a wife. I wanted to argue, but I couldn't. God was keeping me from making a mistake. He showed me that night that my heart was going to bible school to find a wife first, and to prepare myself for ministry second—and that was not going to work.

A few days after this, God spoke to my heart. He said that I was supposed to go to Greater New Orleans Teen Challenge and serve. So I called the director, Greg Dill, and he said that he would love to have me, but there were no staff accommodations at that time. The organization was working on a house next to the center, but for now, I would have to share quarters with the students. To be honest with you, I wasn't looking forward to sleeping on a bunk bed with a bunch of other guys. That had been my living arrangements for almost a year. Nevertheless, when he told me this news, I knew that this was God's plan for me. All my other options were too appealing—God had put it in my heart to answer my calling, not the desires of my flesh.

As it turned out, I was so glad that I went to New Orleans in 1998 and accepted the call.

My Rib

> The Lord God fashioned into a woman the rib which He had
> taken from the man, and brought her to the man. (Genesis 2:22)

> He who finds a wife finds a good thing, and obtains
> favor from the Lord. (Proverbs 18:22)

My best friend in Teen Challenge, Troy, was a joy in my life. When we were in the program together, we were an inspiration to each other. Troy is no longer with us and will be greatly missed, but before he left this world, he would be instrumental in introducing me to my rib.

Six months had passed since graduation, and I was now a staff member at New Orleans Teen Challenge. Life was great. We were getting ready for a graduation ceremony for the guys who had completed the four-month phase, and were on their way to the second phase in Pennsylvania. Troy had called me the day before this graduation and left me a voicemail that said, "I am bringing your rib to the graduation tomorrow night." That was all he had said, and honestly I didn't think a lot of it. Did I desire a wife? Yes, but Troy was a jokester, and sometimes I didn't know when to take him seriously.

That night he brought a friend of his, Sandy, to the graduation. It was that night that I would meet my best friend. Just when I thought life couldn't get any better, God smiled on me. Sandy and I dated for some time, and then married. My mother told me later after we had married she had heard a kind of laughter coming from me that she had not heard since my childhood. Sandy had brought that to my life, and it has not left to this day. Nobody makes me laugh like Sandy, and eleven years later there is no one with whom I would rather spend time. I understand that our wholeness and completeness comes from God, but when He blessed me with Sandy, she was like icing on the cake at last.

She has not only been my best friend, but she understood when we married that she would need to be a part of my call to ministry. She would not change what I knew God had called me to do, but rather, she would realize that she was a part of it.

Sandy was a hair stylist for many years, but about two years after we were married, God was stirring my heart to found a new Teen Challenge in northern Louisiana. It would sit on a twenty-acre facility that had once been a Christian ninety-day program for men struggling with addictions; it had closed, but had been donated to Teen Challenge. If I were to undertake this mission, it would require my wife's leaving her hometown, an eighteen-year hair clientele, and her family. I knew if I was hearing from God, He was going to have to speak to her as well.

Indeed, God spoke to her and confirmed what we were supposed to do. We left our brick home, moved to this property 275 miles away into a twenty-year-old singlewide trailer. Sandy would leave the only profession she ever knew and take a fifty-percent salary cut. God had called her not just to be the spouse of a full-time minister in Teen Challenge, but had called her into full-time ministry as well. That was in 2001. Since 2001, Louisiana Teen Challenge has grown from one residential center in New Orleans housing twelve men to six residential centers housing over one hundred men, women, and families. Thank you, Jesus, for my rib.

REHAB IS NOT FOR THE SOUL

WHERE THE TWELVE STEPS WILL (AND WON'T) TAKE YOU

For the word of the cross is foolishness to those who are perishing, but to us who are being saved it is the power of God. For it is written, I will destroy the wisdom of the wise, and the cleverness of the clever I will set aside. (1 Corinthians 1:18–19)

I have told you about some terrible decisions in my life. I have shared with you my story of redemption. But my passion for writing this book is not to tell you about *my* life—it is to shine a light on what I feel is a mistaken approach to the drug epidemic.

Any attempt to "rehabilitate" someone without the saving power of God is only a temporary fix. Sometimes it is just a substitution of a lesser drug for a greater evil. The world tries one set of medications to get the alcoholic sober, a neurological medication for the one on pain pills, and methadone for the one on heroin. All of these are sad attempts to help the addicted.

Take the methadone maintenance program, for instance. This is a program that is going to help the heroin addict get off of heroin, which is obviously an illegal drug that is destroying thousands of lives. Methadone is an opioid pain reliever similar to morphine. An opioid is sometimes called a narcotic. It also reduces withdrawal symptoms in people addicted to heroin or other narcotic drugs without causing the "high" associated with the drug addiction. Methadone is used as a pain reliever and as part of drug detoxification and maintenance programs (www.drugs.com).

> *Any attempt to "rehabilitate" someone without the saving power of God is only a temporary fix.*

Since joining the ministry of Teen Challenge, I have seen many heroin addicts withdraw. I have also seen them come into our facilities after being on methadone. Trying to withdraw from the methadone is much harder than from heroin—and I have witnessed both. I have had too many calls to count from people who have been on this maintenance program wanting to enter our program, but scared to do so because of the withdrawal. Man's best wisdom is not the answer for the drug epidemic; it never will be. We need to recognize that choosing the lesser of many evils is not the answer, and come to the awakening realization that a power, God, our Creator, the divine person who understands our struggles and wants to help the willing person, is the answer.

The Deceptions and Truths in the Twelve Steps

It is not my goal to be critical of any work that is making a difference. I am speaking from my beliefs and experiences alone, albeit backed by the 86 percent success record of Teen Challenge. In this section, we will be taking a look at the truths in the Twelve Steps, but also the deceptions.

I hope that by examining the positive and negative aspects of the Twelve Steps you will gain a biblical understanding of what is good that can be taken from them. Unfortunately, I know of churches that are taking the Twelve Steps and substituting the name of Jesus for God, which is right—but that is where their changes stop. Those churches and organizations are bringing the world's system in and watering down the Gospel. This keeps the person who yearns for freedom involved in works; the work has already been done through the shed blood of Christ.

The Twelve Steps are probably the most recognized methods of sobriety. We are not seeking for sobriety. We are looking for freedom in Jesus Christ. Some of the Twelve Steps are very biblically sound if they are pointing you in the direction of the Gospel of Jesus Christ. In the sections that follow, I will point these steps out. I will also be pointing out the deceptions, such as the steps pointing you to *God as you understand Him.* If I choose to understand God as Buddha, Mohammed, or any other source other than Jesus Christ, then I am being led astray.

Some steps can have a negative impact on our life, and some will have a positive impact only if the step relates specifically to the Gospel of Jesus Christ as our source of change. It is my responsibility to build up the Gospel and warn the public about the deceptions. It is not my goal to criticize a good effort, but as a minister of the Gospel, I must offer an interpretation from a biblical perspective so that we can see that the finished work of Jesus Christ is enough. The addict does not need a lifestyle of going through steps to remain sober, but a relationship with Jesus Christ to remain free.

STEP 1

> *We admitted we were powerless over our addiction—*
> *that our lives had become unmanageable...*

There is absolutely nothing wrong with this step, if it means that we turn our lives over to Jesus. We do not need to put *all* the emphasis on the addiction, but instead on the fact that we are sinners and addiction is just one of the many sins that are a part of our lives. In other words, I am powerless over my sinful nature and I need to be forgiven of my sins. It is really one big step to Christ, and that is *it*. Now we have eternal life. If I continue in God's word I will remain free of those addictions and the other sin that entangles our lives.

Romans 3:23–24 tells us that "all have sinned, and fall short of the glory of God; being justified freely by his grace through the redemption that is in Christ Jesus.

STEP 2

> *Came to believe that a Power greater than*
> *ourselves could restore us to sanity...*

A Power greater than ourselves... What is this Power? When Bill Wilson began the Twelve Steps years ago, he was someone who was convinced he was powerless over the way his body craved alcohol. He had cried out to God to help him. God had helped Bill get free from addictions and continue to live a sober life. This was not by faith in Jesus Christ, but involved the working of a program.

We are going to look at how the Twelve Steps are helping some people, but based on their works alone. Jesus came and died for our sins so that we do not have to work towards acceptance or deliverance from our bondage. You can work at sobriety through this program and remain sober for fifty years, but not be free. Why? If you do not have faith in

Jesus Christ, you will not go to heaven. Heaven is the ultimate goal for someone serving Jesus Christ. Someone who serves Christ realizes that being sober is just a byproduct of serving Jesus. Being sober should not be the ultimate goal even for someone who has faith in Jesus Christ as his or her Lord and Savior. If being sober remains the main reason for serving God, you could fall short and use again. Our focus as Christians is to love God, and because of our love for Him and His love for us, we are free from anything that would separate us, such as addiction.

Bill believed that a power greater than himself could restore his sanity, but he would not accept Jesus Christ as his Lord and savior. He had to develop steps—works, things to work at, meetings to go to that would keep a person busy. This is not what we want. We need freedom from our addictions through a relationship with Jesus Christ. Bill believed in a power, but what he didn't realize was that his power was his program; his steps are based on human efforts, and those efforts, at best, will fail us. The effort of Jesus and His finished work on the cross will never fail us as long as we trust Him and His word.

Our power as believers is Jesus Christ, himself:

> *So Jesus was saying to those Jews who had believed Him, "If you*
> *continue in My word, then you are truly disciples of Mine; and you*
> *will know the truth, and the truth will make you free." (John 8:31)*

All we have to do is believe in God's word, allow it to abide in our hearts, and we can be free.

STEP 3

> *Made a decision to turn our will and our lives over*
> *to the care of God, as we understood God...*

This is where it gets dangerous. A god can be anything. I was actually taught in the Twelve Step program that this power could be anything. This is often referred to as my "higher power," and if I had faith in a painting or a statue, it could be my god. I know it sounds crazy that some educated people who work at rehabilitation programs lead you in the Twelve Step program could believe that some item in my room could be my higher power. It's true. I experienced it firsthand. The word of God is very clear on idols and any other god placed before Jehovah God in your life. The word of God needs to take precedence over AA's *The Big Book*.

> *And God spake all these words, saying, I am Jehovah thy God, who brought thee out of the land of Egypt, out of the house of bondage. Thou shalt have no other gods before me. Thou shalt not make unto thee a graven image, nor any likeness of anything that is in heaven above, or that is in the earth beneath, or that is in the water under the earth. Thou shalt not bow down thyself unto them, nor serve them, for I Jehovah thy God am a jealous God, visiting the iniquity of the fathers upon the children, upon the third and upon the fourth generation of them that hate me, and showing lovingkindness unto thousands of them that love me and keep my commandments. (Exodus 20:1–6)*

The greatest thing the church has to offer is eternal life in heaven through faith in Jesus Christ. One of the benefits that comes along with that faith is freedom from addictions. Any other method of changing our behavior is a burden we cannot bear. What the addict is looking for in life is freedom, and freedom cannot be found anywhere other than a relationship with Jesus Christ.

Jesus said in Matthew 11: 29–30, "Take my yoke upon you, and learn of me; for I am meek and lowly in heart: and ye shall find rest unto your souls. For my yoke is easy, and my burden is light."

STEP 4

> *Made a searching and fearless moral inventory of ourselves...*

A moral inventory? The AA's *The Big Book* teaches the addict to make a thorough inventory. When I was in rehab, I learned that this was very difficult and painful process if you had lived a life of addiction for many years. What Christ offers us that cannot be gained through our own efforts is this: Once we recognize we are a sinner and accept the forgiveness of Jesus Christ, the Holy Spirit begins to search us and perform the inventory for us.

Search me, O God, and know my heart: Try me, and know
my thoughts; and see if there be any wicked way in me, and
lead me in the way everlasting. (Psalm 139:23–24)

Once again, God has done the work for us. We just have to accept it.

Others and I would really struggle with this step. Without giving your lack of morals to Christ, this process is very self-condemning. Not only that, but once the inventory of this step is done, we have no one to whom to give our pain. Yes, coming to Christ requires us to recognize how filthy we are. We recognize we are sinners in need of a savior. Yet He doesn't require us to do an inventory, and then the Gospel of Jesus Christ gives us forgiveness of our lack of morals.

For what the law could not do, in that it was weak through
the flesh, God, sending his own Son in the likeness of sinful
flesh and for sin, condemned sin in the flesh. (Romans 8:3)

A step like this requires our performance, and Jesus knows that if our success were based on our performance, we would never make it. This is why the addict needs the Gospel. You cannot have a life of freedom based on your performance; you must also have the grace and forgiveness of Jesus Christ.

Seek ye Jehovah while he may be found; call ye upon him
while he is near: Let the wicked forsake his way, and the
unrighteous man his thoughts; and let him return unto
Jehovah, and he will have mercy upon him; and to our
God, for he will abundantly pardon. (Isaiah 55:6–7)

This is what God offers the addict: a pardon! There is no system or series of steps that can offer this promise of pardon to the addict. All we have to do is come to Christ as a sinner and recognize that addiction is a sin, and you will be forgiven. You do not have to do an inventory. The bible says in Jeremiah 1:5, "Before I formed thee in the belly I knew thee."

So Christ knows us and has known us from the beginning. There is no need for me to tell Him all the bad I have done. He knows, and all I have to confess is affirm that I am a sinner and I want to be forgiven.

STEP 5

> *Admitted to God, to ourselves, and to another human*
> *being the exact nature of our wrongs…*

> *This is perhaps difficult, especially discussing our defects with another*
> *person. We think we have done well enough in admitting these things*
> *to ourselves. There is doubt about that. In actual practice, we usually*
> *find a solitary self-appraisal insufficient. Many of us thought it*
> *necessary to go much further. We will be more reconciled to discussing*
> *ourselves with another person when we see good reasons why we*
> *should do so. The best reason first: If we skip this vital step, we may*
> *not overcome drinking. Time after time newcomers have tried to*
> *keep to themselves certain facts about their lives. Trying to avoid*
> *this humbling experience, they have turned to easier methods. Almost*
> *invariably they got drunk. Having persevered with the rest of the*
> *program, they wondered why they fell. We think the reason is that they*
> *never completed their housecleaning. They took inventory all right, but*
> *hung on to some of the worst items in stock. They only thought they*
> *had lost their egoism and fear; they only thought they had humbled*
> *themselves. But they had not learned enough of humility, fearlessness*
> *and honesty, in the sense we find it necessary, until they told*
> *someone else their entire life story.* (AA, *The Big Book, p. 72–73*)

It's great to tell your story to other people, but to have telling that story be a part of your sobriety adds an unhelpful perspective to the process of change. In other words, it's unhelpful to think, "If I don't get this story told in detail to somebody, I will probably drink again." That is not a way to live.

> *And they overcame him because of the blood of the Lamb, and*
> *because of the word of their testimony.* (*Revelation 12:11*)

As believers in Christ, we are promised that we are overcomers by the word of our testimony. Letting people know what Christ has done in our life is a vital part of our walk; but that does not involve me sitting down with a person and telling them my story in detail as a part of my sobriety. As forgiven sinners desiring to remain free, our testimony is letting people know on a continual basis, "Once I was a bad sinner, but now I have been pardoned and been forgiven since the day Jesus sacrificed his life for all of my sins."

> *How much more shall the blood of Christ, who through the eternal Spirit offered himself without blemish unto God, cleanse your conscience from dead works to serve the living God? And for this cause he is the mediator of a new covenant, that a death having taken place for the redemption of the transgressions that were under the first covenant, they that have been called may receive the promise of the eternal inheritance. (Hebrews 9:14)*

We cannot place our hope in being free from addiction by telling my detailed life story to an individual. We need to continually tell others the story of Jesus Christ. Tell others we have been redeemed because of His shed blood.

STEP 6

> *We're entirely ready to have God remove all these defects of character...*

As Christians, we need to be ready to have Jesus remove all of our character defects. Our walk with Jesus is a process, and He will continue to work things out in our life; if we do not allow them to be worked out, they could become defects and cause us problems later. I am not talking about addiction; we are assuming that Jesus has removed this problem. After we turn our lives over to Jesus, we submit to a process of sanctification, and grow in God's grace. Whatever major vice was keeping us from Christ—whether it was substance abuse, gambling, pornography, or adultery—God will immediately take it away and then set us on the road towards His Grace. The word of God tells us He will bring us from glory to glory, that is, a greater understanding of Grace from one day to the next.

A good illustration of this is in Romans 5:1–5.

Therefore, having been justified by faith, we have peace with
God through our Lord Jesus Christ, through whom also we
have obtained our introduction by faith into this grace in
which we stand; and we exult in hope of the glory of God. And
not only this, but we also exult in our tribulations, knowing
that tribulation brings about perseverance; and perseverance,
proven character; and proven character, hope; and hope does not
disappoint, because the love of God has been poured out within
our hearts through the Holy Spirit who was given to us.

Our defects of character are going to be removed from our life as we allow the Holy Spirit to reveal these to us.

Search me, O God, and know my heart; try me and know
my anxious thoughts; and see if there be any hurtful way in
me, and lead me in the everlasting way. (Psalm 139:23–24)

This was King David asking God to search him and let him know if there was anything in his life that needed to go. Let it be your daily prayer Jesus. *Search me.* This can only be done by the piercing power of the Holy Spirit. We are not able to sit down with our own thoughts, and with our own strength and power, tell God what's wrong. We need Him to tell us what's wrong—after all, He knows us. This was God's response to Jacob when he was questioning the guidance he received:

Thus says the Lord who made you, and formed you from the womb,
who will help you, do not fear Jacob my servant. (Isaiah 44:2)

The word of God also tells us in Jeremiah 1:5, "Before I formed you in the womb I knew you." This is who we need doing our moral inventory: our Designer, our Creator. If your Ford car was broken and your choice was either a shade-tree mechanic or Henry Ford for the same price, whom would you choose?

STEP 7

Humbly asked God to remove our shortcomings…

This step can be a continual part of a believer's life. Not just the ex-addict, but anyone who has trusted Jesus Christ as their Savior. The bible tells us in Romans 3:23–24, "For all have sinned and fall short of the glory of God, being justified as a gift by His grace through the redemption which is in Christ Jesus."

We all have sins and shortcomings that we will struggle with daily. It is our responsibility as Christians to humbly come before God and ask Him to cleanse us, and He does just that.

> *I acknowledged my sin to You, and my iniquity I did not*
> *hide; I said, I will confess my transgressions to the Lord;*
> *and You forgave the guilt of my sin. (Psalm 32:5)*

> *If we confess our sins, He is faithful and righteous to forgive*
> *us our sins and to cleanse us from all unrighteousness. If*
> *we say that we have not sinned, we make Him a*
> *liar and His word is not in us. (1 John 1:9–10)*

This needs to be a part of a believer's life, giving all our shortcomings to Him, recognizing that in Christ we can be better people than we were yesterday. We have to take care not to condemn ourselves as we approach God with our faults, but that we are doing the opposite—freeing ourselves. God wants to replace all our shortcomings with His character. It's a process. Once we are born again and filled with His spirit, the process begins. At any time we fall short, we have an advocate, Jesus Christ, who died and will forgive us of that failure; but more important, He will empower us with the grace to succeed where we have failed before.

STEPS 8 AND 9

> *Made a list of all persons we had harmed, and*
> *became willing to make amends to them all…*

> *Made direct amends to such people wherever possible,*
> *except when to do so would injure them or others…*

During my many stays in Twelve Step–based rehab programs, these two were steps that I was never able to complete. Many other people struggled because of them, and ultimately gave up and fell. As I would begin to make a list, I would start feeling terrible about harming so many people, and rightly so. In some cases, making amends would require offering reimbursement for something we stole, apologizing to someone we hurt, and so forth—but for me, to make amends to all after eighteen years of addiction was unreasonable and set me up for failure. If we look only to the forgiveness that other people offer us—or don't offer—then we will start gauging our sense of forgiveness by their reactions to us, and that is a recipe for failure.

The only reparation we need to strive for is the one with Jesus Christ. We must embrace only the truth that He has already forgiven us. Without that, self-forgiveness is impossible. Please do not misunderstand; we do need to acknowledge the wrong we have done and give it to God. Trust that He is going to lead us, His new creation, in the right direction at the right time to make amends to the right people.

Finally, trying to make a list of everyone we have harmed as a part of our recovery entrusts our recovery to our own limited abilities. It was our best efforts and abilities that brought us failure. It is now time to realize who we are in Christ, and trust in Christ. Through Him, we obtain freedom, and recognize that in Christ, we are more than conquerors!

STEP 10

> *Continued to take personal inventory and when*
> *we were wrong promptly admitted it...*

As we mentioned earlier concerning Step 4, we are not capable of doing a moral inventory. We are by nature bad; no one had to teach us as a child to lie to our parents about breaking the lamp on the nightstand. It came naturally. We do not need our natural humanity doing inventory for us. We need God to continue to search our heart.

> *The heart is more deceitful than all else, and is desperately sick; who*
> *can understand it? I, the Lord, search the heart. (Jeremiah 17:9)*

STEP 11

> *Sought through prayer and meditation to improve our conscious*
> *contact with God as we understood God, praying only for*
> *knowledge of God's will for us and the power to carry that out...*

There is only one way to God and that is through His son Jesus Christ. In John 14:66 Jesus said to him, "I am the way, and the truth, and the life; no one comes to the Father but through Me."

If you understand God to be anything other than Jesus Christ, then contemplate the Scripture.

> *My little children, I am writing these things to you so that*
> *you may not sin. And if anyone sins, we have an Advocate*
> *with the Father, Jesus Christ the righteous; and He Himself*
> *is the propitiation for our sins; and not for ours only, but*
> *also for those of the whole world. (1 John 2:1–2)*

Prayer, meditation, desiring to improve our relationship with God needs to be a continual part of the believer's life. Ephesians 6:18 says, "With all prayer and petition pray at all times in the Spirit."

The bible calls us to prayer. Not praying and meditating on God's word is to neglect one of the greatest gifts that God bestowed on His children. It's like when you are a child and you are able to cry and let your parents know that you are hungry. Then you grow older and you are able to talk and let them know exactly what you need. Even if you don't know exactly what you need from your parents, good, loving parents know what you need even when you don't. And so it is with God. He knows what we need. Yes, He wants to speak to us, and a large part of our prayer life does need to be just simply listening. We need to spend time not being anxious, letting God know how grateful we are for who He is in our life, and He guarantees us peace. Peace is what we all are chasing in life. Let's apply the scripture to our life and walk in peace that surpasses all understanding.

We need God's help so that we enter not into temptation.

Be anxious for nothing, but in everything by prayer and supplication
with thanksgiving let your requests be made known to God. And
the peace of God, which surpasses all comprehension, will guard
your hearts and your minds in Christ Jesus. (Philippians 4:6–7)

Pray that you will not enter into temptation.

When He rose from prayer, He came to the disciples and found them
sleeping from sorrow, and said to them, Why are you sleeping? Get up
and pray that you may not enter into temptation. (Luke 22:45–46)

Jesus was encouraging His disciples to pray that they would not enter
into temptation. We are no different. We need God's help so that we
enter not into temptation.

Before I gave my life to Christ, I not only struggled with drugs and
alcohol. Pornography is a part of my past, as well. Shortly after I was
married, I was on my way to work at Teen Challenge in New Orleans.
It was a normal drive to work, and then out of nowhere, as I passed an
adult video store that I had passed many times before, I was struck by
a demonic temptation to pull into the video store. I always listened to
the bible on cassette during my commute. When this temptation came
over me, I really didn't know what to pray. I prayed, groaning in the spirit,
and it was only a couple of minutes later that the narrator on the cassette
bible spoke these words:

Drink water from your own cistern and fresh water from your own
well. Should your springs be dispersed abroad, streams of water
in the streets? Let them be yours alone and not for strangers with
you. Let your fountain be blessed, and rejoice in the wife of your
youth. As a loving hind and a graceful doe, let her breasts satisfy
you at all times; be exhilarated always with her love. For why
should you, my son, be exhilarated with an adulteress and embrace
the bosom of a foreigner? For the ways of a man are before the eyes
of the Lord, and He watches all his paths. (Proverbs 5:15–21)

Some people may say this was a coincidence, but I don't believe it. I believe it was God taking care of His child who was asking Him for help. Pray without ceasing.

> *Pray without ceasing; in everything give thanks; for this is God's will for you in Christ Jesus. (1 Thessalonians 5:17–18)*

STEP 12

> *Having had a spiritual awakening as the result of these steps, we tried to carry this message to other addicts, and to practice these principles in all our affairs.*

We should not rely on secular steps to lead us to a spiritual awakening. Our spiritual awakening comes only through the grace of God. When I think back on the "emotional experience" that I was told I had in my first rehab, I recognize that moment as a spiritual awakening that was put to sleep—a deep spiritual opportunity diverted into the shallow waters of secular recovery. So many years later, I worked my way into the freedom that only Christ can offer. My spiritual awakening came in Orleans Parish Prison as a result of reading God's word and being drawn by His Spirit.

> *But what does it say? The word is near you, in your mouth and in your heart—that is, the word of faith which we are preaching, that if you confess with your mouth Jesus as Lord, and believe in your heart that God raised Him from the dead, you will be saved; for with the heart a person believes, resulting in righteousness, and with the mouth he confesses, resulting in salvation. For the Scripture says, Whoever believes in Him will not be disappointed. (Romans 10:8–11)*

> *No one can come to Me unless the Father who sent Me draws him. (John 6:44)*

Our awakening lies totally in being convinced that Jesus is who He claims to be, accepting his identity, and making God's word a part of our life. After that awakening, we can take hold of all that God has promised for His children.

As a partaker of God's grace, I testify that this is a message we need to carry to the world. It is necessary for our spiritual wellbeing to carry the message of grace.

> *And they overcame him because of the blood of the Lamb and*
> *because of the word of their testimony. (Revelation 12:11)*

Someone who has been restored to Christ has been given the responsibility of ministry. Helping others and bringing people to the saving knowledge of our Lord and Savior Jesus Christ—this keeps us alive.

> *Therefore if anyone is in Christ, he is a new creature; the old*
> *things passed away; behold, new things have come. Now all*
> *these things are from God, who reconciled us to Himself through*
> *Christ and gave us the ministry of reconciliation, namely,*
> *that God was in Christ reconciling the world to Himself, not*
> *counting their trespasses against them, and He has committed*
> *to us the word of reconciliation. (2 Corinthians 5:17)*

The Church Has the Answer

> *Holding a form of godliness, but having*
> *denied the power... (2 Timothy 3:5)*

I was raised in church. I can remember going to church on Wednesday nights with my Mom for choir rehearsal. We were there on Sunday mornings and sometimes on Sunday nights, especially if we had something going on for the youth group. I do not intend to criticize any church, its fellowship, or its parishioners. I can say, however, that I witnessed—and continue to witness—bodies of Christians gathering in Christ, yet not believing that God is the answer for their problems. Whether it is their problems, their friend's problems, or family members' problems, God *is* the answer.

We continue to believe that addiction can be cured by someone who has enough knowledge about addiction. That person can be a medical doctor who can prescribe the right medication. It can be an educated psychiatrist who can dig for the deep-rooted emotional issue that is causing the addicted person to use drugs or alcohol. All of these are indeed assets, but the church has the answer! The answer is a relationship with Jesus Christ, supported by a lifestyle tailored to the word of God, and guided by the Holy Spirit. Wherever God-seeking gets second fiddle to any other sort of effort, the chance of freedom is slim. Even if he or she can get sober, with no relationship with God, life will not be fulfilling.

Too many churches have a form of godliness, but deny its transformative power. As long we continue to put our faith in secular treatment, we do a great injustice to anyone struggling with addiction. Right now, right this minute, the church has the answer. If a Christian just has a form of godliness but denies the delivering power of God, then this vital message is likely to be lost in translation.

Years ago, during my own battles, not many people in the church told me that Jesus could help me with my addiction. They were always looking to secular programs, therapy, and treatment to fix me. Now, I encourage people to believe that the Creator of this universe knows our struggles and knows how to fix it. We just have to acknowledge and allow Him to take charge.

THE REHAB ATTEMPTS

As we have looked at the Twelve Steps, you now have a better understanding of our secular rehabs. They're a money-making industry whose track record of success pales beside the record of Teen Challenge. In this chapter, we will cover the lies I have heard with my own ears, and steer ourselves toward the only program that matters: The program of loving God with all our hearts.

Lie: "Relapse Is Part of Recovery."

This lesson that relapse is part of recovery was really made popular when the NA (Narcotics Anonymous) book was written. NA was started to cater to the drug addict. There was really no difference in the steps, but the book and the meetings were geared toward the drug addict. Before that split, it was often comical to notice how alcoholics would look down on the drug addicts, and the drug addicts would look down on the alcoholics. Like one sin was worse. They really needed separate meetings, and so it began. Later on they started CA (cocaine anonymous) to cater to the cocaine addict. Many more have been started to address whatever addiction you had.

I can remember reading that relapse was a part of recovery and asking at meetings if it really meant what it said. Other members would confirm that using again after you come to a meeting and start the Twelve Steps is a part of your recovery. They didn't encourage it,

God will take away addictions immediately, if we want to give them to Him.

but it was accepted as normal. They would tell you just keep coming back to the program after using.

When you give your heart to Jesus Christ and desire to be free from addictions, I believe we have one teaching and one teaching only, John 8:34–36.

> *Jesus answered them, Truly, truly, I say to you, everyone*
> *who commits sin is the slave of sin. The slave does not*
> *remain in the house forever; the son does remain forever. So*
> *if the Son makes you free, you will be free indeed.*

When we give our life to Christ He starts working on us and we start to grow.,

> *Like newborn babies, long for the pure milk of the word, so*
> *that by it you may grow in respect to salvation, if you*
> *have tasted the kindness of the Lord. (1 Peter 2:2–3)*

I understand what they are trying to say at meetings—but as a Christian who is free now, I can't accept their reasoning. Nor do I want to see others accept it. You have no idea where your next binge may take you. It could be death. I believe with all my heart that there are some things in our lives, like addictions, that God will take away immediately if we want to give them to Him. He knows these vices will keep us bound, unable to grow in the Lord. If we are not able to move on, we can never grow to the level of maturity in Christ that assures total freedom.

As a Christian who was once addicted, let me tell you that using again is not part of my walk with Christ. It is not a part of anybody's walk with Christ. If you happen to slip as a Christian, you have a heavenly Father who will forgive you and all you have to do is repent and ask for forgiveness, and move on. Acts 3:19 says, "Therefore repent and return, so that your sins may be wiped away, in order that times of refreshing may come from the presence of the Lord." God does not require you to go back to an AA or NA meeting and pick up your twenty-four hour chip after you have been clean for let's say eight months, thereby letting everyone there know that you have fallen. That's a very hard thing to do. It can bring on condemnation, and the word of God tells us in Romans 8:1–2, "Therefore there is now no condemnation for those who are in

Christ Jesus. For the law of the Spirit of life in Christ Jesus has set you free from the law of sin and of death."

Relapse is not a part of recovery. Jesus wants us to live free, and if we fall short, He wants to pick us up and restore us to the point at which we left off, so that we may continue our journey in the Lord.

Lie: "My Name Is Gary, and I Am an Alcoholic."

At the beginning of the book I shared with you an experience in my first rehab, a motivation for writing this book. When I completed rehab, I wanted to succeed by applying the principles I had been taught. One of the requirements to be successful was I needed to make ninety AA meetings in ninety days.

When I first heard this, I was like, "That's pretty cool—sounds like a neat goal to reach." There were problems, though. I didn't have transportation, and I had to rely on my parents to take me to these meetings, which became a burden on all of us. They have given me a goal, and in my mind, if I did not reach the goal, I was guaranteed to fail.

The meetings I attended were very depressing. At these meetings, we would gather around and smoke cigarettes. Sometimes a guest speaker would share war stories about drinking. The guest was always an alcoholic telling us how they had not had anything to drink that day. It seemed to me that I was listening to someone that was not free. I would come away from hearing the guest speaker with the feeling they were one bad decision away from being a full-blown drunk again. I remember feeling that there had to be something more.

Another of my post-rehab, assigned goals was to get a sponsor, someone to talk to whenever I felt like I had the urge to drink. If I could do that, and at the same time continue to work the Twelve Steps, I would have a chance of remaining sober. Something just did not seem right. This was a burden I felt I couldn't bear—the meetings, working the steps, the sponsor.

The meetings I needed were to attend church and celebrate my freedom with Christ with other believers. The steps I needed to work were reading God's word on how to live everyday life. My sponsor needed to be Jesus Christ, who knows me better than anybody, and who will always be there when I need him. He will never fail me! As well-meaning as a sponsor may be in a program like AA, they are human and it is impossible for them to fill your needs, meet your expectations, and have all the right words to say when you are backed against a wall by an acute desire to use. Jesus always knows what to say through His word, and will take you to freedom—a place where you will not need a drink so much that you would have to call somebody.

> *Therefore if anyone is in Christ, he is a new creature; the old things passed away; behold, new things have come. (2 Corinthians 5:17)*

This is our promise as a believer the old is gone; the new has come!

"My name is Gary, and I am an alcoholic and a drug addict." That is how we were told to introduce ourselves at a meeting. The bible tells us there is power in our words...

> *Look at the ships also, though they are so great and are driven by strong winds, are still directed by a very small rudder wherever the inclination of the pilot desires. So also the tongue is a small part of the body, and yet it boasts of great things. (James 3:4–5)*

This was definitely not what I would call speaking life over myself. I was telling myself I was an alcoholic and a drug addict, and would always be one. I was telling myself that my only salvation would be the meetings, my sponsor, and the steps. The word of God tells us that in Christ we have accepted by faith that Christ died for our sins; that we are no longer an alcoholic or a drug addict, but instead are new creations in Christ. My response now is, "My name is Gary, and I was once an alcoholic and a drug addict—a sinner, but now I am free. That man is dead and the new Gary will never have to fall back into that lifestyle again."

Lie: "Sharing Your Feelings Will Cure You."

I made the mistake of getting involved with a girl who was already dating a black belt in karate. I was very drunk when he came to my hotel room late one night to confront me. Now, I didn't know she was involved with someone else, and honestly did not consider myself involved with her. We had met in a bar and partied together a couple of nights. But her boyfriend came to the room to inform me she was his girlfriend, and before I knew it, he had given me a karate kick to the nose. Results: broken nose and the black eyes that go along with a broken nose.

There was a lot of bleeding due to the broken nose, so I called the ambulance and ended up being admitted to the hospital—not because of my broken nose, but due to my blood alcohol content. My body was saturated with alcohol. The doctor asked if I wanted some help and that he could get me in somewhere. So I checked into a state-run six-month rehabilitation program. I really did want to change. I thought I did, any-way. Looking back, I really am not sure. After sobering up, one of my first experiences in this program was a meeting where all the clients gathered around in a circle and the counselor would pick someone to sit in the middle of the circle to be questioned.

They called me to sit in the chair in the middle of this circle that was surrounded by about thirty clients and one counselor. I was nervous. Some of them called this the cocaine podium and this is where you were going to get confronted by the other clients in the program. That never made sense to me. The first question asked was how I got my black eyes. I began to tell them the story behind the black eyes, and before I could finish, they were calling me a liar. The counselor had told me I was lying. All the clients agreed I was lying. It was one of the few times in recent history that I was actually telling the truth. They also were using curse words at a high volume to let me know I was lying and I needed to be honest with myself. They could see that I was getting upset with all of these false accusations as they all had their own theory as to how I received the black eyes. The counselor stepped in and said, "How does this make you feel?" I responded with, "I don't know." Well, that was the wrong answer, and it started the next wave of comments from the circle. "Why don't you know how you feel?" I was so mad about being called a liar that I couldn't move on to getting in touch with my feelings.

Since I could not tell them how I felt, the counselor asked me to stand up in my chair, tuck my hands under my armpits, squat down and flap my arms while clucking like a chicken. I participated in this humiliating activity, and then he asked me, "How do you feel?" I told him, "Like an idiot!"

He said, "See, you can tell us how you feel." This was the beginning of my treatment, to be called a liar, have insults thrown at me, and to act

like a human chicken. This was an example of man's best wisdom to help
me overcome my addictions. Needless to say, it didn't help, and to this
day I believe that it was all foolishness to God.

Lie: "We Will Tear You Down to Build You Up."

It was called Monday Morning Big Group. All the clients would gather
in a circle. This was a very large circle. It was everyone in the program
at the time, men and women. With hardly any words spoken, the staff
would come down and stand by the circle looking at it like they were
analyzing all of us. They gazed at us like we were prey and they were
the lions ready to pounce. The director of the program and the head
counselor would begin to pace around the circle looking at the clients. It
was a very nerve-wracking time. About two or three minutes into their
pace around the client circle, they would tap a client on the shoulder and
say, "Go pack your stuff."

That client would then get up, and one of the other staff would escort
him or her upstairs, and that would be the end of the program. This was
done with no explanation at all. The staff may have given an explanation
after they were upstairs, but at the meeting when you were told to "go
pack your stuff," you were given none. This would happen to maybe three
or four clients every Monday morning. It's one thing to dismiss someone
from the program, but this was done in a cruel way.

I did find out later that all these decisions were made based on notes
the weekend monitors had taken about clients' activity and misbehavior
over the weekend. It was not talked about with the client. They were not
warned about what they may have done wrong; they were just told to
leave.

This is how educated people employed by the state approached people's lives. These were clients who came in broken down. A lot of secular
treatment facilities believe they need to tear the person down even further before they start working on them. I guess that is their best wisdom.
They don't have faith that Jesus Christ is the one that can humble, strip
someone of their pride, and then supernaturally build them up and restore them. We all do only what we know to do.

Lie: "Follow Your Sponsor's Example."

Upon completion of the rehab that had me clucking like a chicken, I went to a halfway house, continued working the Twelve Steps, and looked for a job. The goal at the halfway house was to find a job and save money to get your own apartment and transportation. One of the things they stress in working the Twelve Steps is to find a sponsor, someone whom you can call when you feel like using. I was taking this very seriously and was attending meetings and talking to potential sponsors. This needed to be someone who had been sober for a long period of time.

After attending several meetings, I met a guy who said he hadn't had a drink in fifteen years and was a car salesman. That really excited me, and I felt like this was going to be my sponsor. This had to be the guy. I approached him and asked if he would be my sponsor, and he accepted. This really encouraged me, because I really wanted a better life for myself.

He was a very nice man and even offered to come by the halfway house and give me a ride to meetings. We would go to meetings and sometimes get something to eat. We were building a good relationship, one that I felt I could bare my soul and talk about anything. One night on the way back to the halfway house from a meeting, he bared his soul with me. It was a moment that changed my course through this secular system. He told me he had not drunk alcohol for fifteen years, but confessed that on occasions he would smoke marijuana to help him with his stress.

Jesus was and is perfect...You never have to worry about Him leading you astray.

I was speechless. I didn't know what to say. Emotions were running rampant and I told myself that this is the program they gave me, and so this sponsor must know what he is talking about. I accepted his doctrine, his way of working the program, and honestly it's exactly what *I wanted to hear.*

You are My friends if you do what I command you. No longer do I call you slaves, for the slave does not know what his master is

doing; but I have called you friends, for all things that I have heard
from My Father I have made known to you. (John 15:14–15)

Jesus was and is perfect. All of our counsel comes from His living word.
You never have to worry about Him leading you astray.

Lie: "You Can Take a Moral Inventory of Yourself."

Search me, O God, and know my heart; try me and know my anxious
thoughts; and see if there be any hurtful way in me. (Psalm 139:23–24)

Sometimes we don't even know what our agenda is. I believe this was the
case for me when I checked into the Salvation Army adult rehabilitation
program. They really have a great organization, and I am grateful for the
leadership at this ministry. As I look back on my stay at this program,
there were some things that were missing. One was that I had deceit in
my heart, and didn't even know it.

There was a part of me, a large part of me, which really wanted to
be different. I thought I was doing all that was necessary to facilitate
change. I was doing everything they asked me at the Salvation Army. I
was a hard worker, and I participated sincerely in the chapel services and
devotions.

Even though the program was attempting to offer us spiritual change,
the one thing that they did not enforce was a smoking ban. I continued
to smoke while I was in the program, which does not give the drug addict
or alcoholic much of a chance at deliverance. Eventually the program's
major started giving me some responsibility and made me manager over
the adjacent thrift store. I was always a hard worker and loved new chal-
lenges, so I came up with some creative ideas that increased business.

The major really liked the job I was doing. One day he called me
into his office and wanted to know my long-term plans. I told him that
I really didn't have any. He informed me that he would like me to take
over supervising five Salvation Army thrift stores around the city. I was
flattered, excited, and eager for the challenge.

What about the reason I was in the program? What about my addictions? What about the wrecked life that showed up at the program
doorstep a few months earlier? Honestly, none of it came up in that

conversation. I did not have a relationship with God that would enable me to ask Him to search my heart and show me if there was any wicked way in me. My deceptive heart had not been born anew, and it was going to lead me astray again.

Not long after I was given the responsibility for running the stores, I started taking money from the deposits. Just a little at a time so it would go unnoticed. That's right—I was stealing from a ministry. To this day, I feel so awful about what I did. This went on for a few months and my goal was to buy a car. Not to use drugs, but to buy a car with stolen money. I had justified in my mind that this was okay.

What happened next was that I spent the money instead on a one-weekend binge. I used drugs and ended up homeless on the streets again.

That is how deceitful the heart is. As much as I wanted to do right, I lacked the conviction and power of God in my life that would have shown me the deception that remained in my heart. The secular treatment programs tell us to do a moral inventory of ourselves. We are not capable of doing a moral inventory. It can only be done by willingly welcoming God's scrutiny of our hearts. Only God can do an inventory.

Once we have turned our lives over to Jesus Christ, like David, we must pray, "Search me, O God, and know my heart; try me and know my anxious thoughts; and see if there be any hurtful way in me."

Truth: Secular Treatment Offers No Eternity

> *He who has found his life will lose it, and he who has lost*
> *his life for My sake will find it. (Matthew 10:39)*

These are the words of Jesus and He is talking about losing your life on this earth so that we can have eternal life with Him in heaven. Heaven is real; eternal life is real. The only way we can spend eternity in heaven is acknowledging that we are sinners, and accept the fact that Jesus died for our sins and rose again. It's my belief that if I am able to get someone sober, but they die without eternal life, what good did I do?

For what will it profit a man if he gains the whole
world and forfeits his soul? Or what will a man give
in exchange for his soul? (Matthew 16:26)

What good is a sober life without the knowledge of God's eternity? It is just that—just a sober life. I continue to tell students in Teen Challenge that I am not concerned with their substance abuse problems; I am concerned about their eternal destination.

He who believes in the Son has eternal life; but he who
does not obey the Son will not see life. (John 3:36)

I know that if we can get someone's heart set on the eternal—a benefit of accepting Jesus as his or her Savior—then that person will not have to worry about a drug problem because the word of God tells us in John 8:36, "So if the Son makes you free, you will be free indeed."

We need to put our focus on the eternal not only to live a life free from addiction, but to motivate our prayer life for our friends and family. We need to be driven by eternity to pray for and help those who need freedom from addiction. As long as our main motivation is the temporal—months and years of sobriety—our priorities are out of order. If we are serving God to be free of drugs, not drink again, save our marriage, and so forth, that will not sustain us. If we are serving God because He loves us and we love Him, then we have eternal life because our sins are forgiven. If we understand that a fruit of His Grace is sobriety then our priorities are in order. It's perfectly okay and normal for life's problems to necessitate the grace of God in our lives, but at some point that must change. We must recognize that God has taken care of those problems. We should eventually say of them, "They are no longer a part of my life, and I am moving from glory to glory."

> *I am not concerned with students' substance abuse problems; I am concerned about their eternal destination.*

But we all, with unveiled face, beholding as in a mirror the glory of the Lord, are being transformed into the same image from glory to glory, just as from the Lord, the Spirit. (2 Corinthians 3:18)

In other words, now that the veil has been lifted, we recognize that we are sinners; God is now showing us who we are apart from His grace, and are being transformed. This is a process of becoming more and more like our Savior. The hope of the addicted person and of those who are praying for the addicted is that he or she will come to a revelation that God wants us to move *past* our deliverance from addiction and focus on the eternal. As we pray for and minister to those who are addicted, I believe we present the Gospel more effectively if we focus on eternity. And as we focus on eternity, we are brought from glory to glory in our walk.

PRINCIPLES OF SUCCESS

God is not one to show partiality. (*Acts 10:34*)

I could preach a fifteen-year sermon to you. But instead, what I want to do is share with you some biblical principles that God has shown me over the last fifteen years—principles that have helped me continue to grow in His grace, and will help the once-addicted grow in His grace, too.

Anybody can make it. I know this because I have been living a successful life for fifteen years, totally free from addictions. Not only that, but am living a life blessed by God. I am married to a woman who loves God, and we both work together in full-time ministry. I serve as the chief operating officer in the ministry of Louisiana Teen Challenge. The trick is that when you feel life's pressures, you take those pressures and trials and turn them over to God, and learn from them. So even from the life's normal ups and downs, I have remained free.

The word of God tells me that God does not show partiality. In the following chapters of this book, I share with you some biblical principles that can help anyone walk free from any life-controlling substance.

No Nicotine

Addiction is addiction. I am not saying, "Once an addict always an addict," as some secular treatment centers do. But for someone who has been delivered from drugs and alcohol, why hang on to a nicotine addiction? It is a physical addiction, and God does not want you to struggle with such a burden.

Treatment centers that work the Twelve Steps will actually encourage you to keep smoking so that you are not struggling to quit all

Anything that is damaging to our body pollutes our temple.

of your addictions at once. That's the problem! We cannot "quit" these addictions. When we are physically addicted, and God has not set us free, then we must rely on our strength alone, and we are setting ourselves up for failure. That is a task that we cannot handle. We need the power and grace of God to take those addictions away.

> *Do you not know that you are a temple of God and that*
> *the Spirit of God dwells in you? If any man destroys the*
> *temple of God, God will destroy him, for the temple of God is*
> *holy, and that is what you are. (1 Corinthians 3:16–17)*

When we turn our lives over to Jesus Christ, His Spirit fills us and our body is literally filled with God's Holy Spirit. Not just nicotine, but anything that is damaging to our body, pollutes our temple. God desires us to abstain. We can never accomplish perfection in our flesh, but we can choose to give the things we know are wrong to God. We must give Him a clean temple to dwell. We want to follow the example of Jesus and the CEO of Louisiana Teen Challenge: Reverend Greg Dill once said, "Could you imagine Jesus giving that great sermon of the beatitudes while smoking a Camel or chewing on some Levi Garret?"

I have been with Louisiana Teen Challenge for fifteen years and have seen hundreds come through our doors. We do not allow tobacco at our facilities, and I have not yet seen a single person who is living a successful, addiction-free life in Christ decide to pick up cigarettes after graduation. I often tell students, "Is this a statistic that you would want to be a part of?" God has called us to holiness.

> *But like as he who called you is holy, be ye yourselves also*
> *holy in all manner of living; because it is written, Ye*
> *shall be holy; for I am holy. (1 Peter 1:15)*

Be Accountable

> *Iron sharpens iron, so one man sharpens another. (Proverbs 27:17)*

We need accountability. We need people who will love and care enough about our wellbeing to ask us tough questions; people to whom we can give honest answers. Every believer must embrace this principle—especially the believer who was delivered from addictions. If your pride is getting in the way of allowing someone into your life, you must pray about it.

> *Brethren, even if anyone is caught in any trespass, you who are spiritual, restore such a one in a spirit of gentleness; each one looking to yourself, so that you too will not be tempted. Bear one another's burdens, and thereby fulfill the law of Christ. For if anyone thinks he is something when he is nothing, he deceives himself.* (Galatians 6:1–3)

A person to whom we are accountable can be trusted to say something to us if they see us involved in sin. Not just a sin such as drinking or adultery—but also sins of arrogance and pride. If they see these sins, they should be willing to pray with us in love.

After completing one of the rehabs, I went to a halfway house where I was going to work a job, go to AA meetings, save money, and get an apartment, all the while remaining sober. Two weeks after receiving my first check from my employer, I went on a crack binge. Two days later, on a Sunday afternoon, I called the halfway house hoping to receive grace and come back. The staff member invited me to return and to write the director a letter explaining to him where I went wrong and what I was going to do differently. I wrote him a letter that was full of what I hoped he would want to hear—honestly, I just didn't want to be kicked out on the streets. I spent half the night on this letter and was very proud of it.

The church is where you will meet friends for life, friends who will support you, pray with you, and cry with you.

Monday morning seemed to pass in slow motion as I waited for the director to come into work. He finally showed up and called me into his office. He told me he didn't believe a word of what I had written. I was furious. But for the first time in my life, *somebody saw right through me.*

He was not a Christian and neither was I, but there is a biblical truth to this story.

We must ask God to place the right people in our lives—people who can hold us accountable by pointing out, in love, the sins that exist in our blind spots. We don't need a sponsor in AA who will tell us that smoking pot is okay; we need men and women that love God and will pray for us, men and women who believe in us, "not forsaking our own assembling together, as is the habit of some, but encouraging one another; and all the more as you see the day drawing near" (Hebrews 10:25).

Furthermore, be accountable to your church. Be faithful in church. The church is where you will meet friends for life, friends who will support you, pray with you, and cry with you. The church is where you will find your brothers and sisters in the Lord. If someone is faithful to their church, and if they miss a couple of Sundays, somebody will call them to see if everything is okay—I don't know how many times I have seen this happen. It's not a matter of micro-managing another person's life, but just being concerned about them. Your church does not need to be someone you listen to on TV, either. Although that is fine, we need a body of believers who are in fellowship with us on a weekly basis, a family.

> *Two are better than one because they have a good return for their labor. For if either of them falls, the one will lift up his companion. But woe to the one who falls when there is not another to lift him up. Furthermore, if two lie down together they keep warm, but how can one be warm alone? And if one can overpower him who is alone, two can resist him. A cord of three strands is not quickly torn apart. (Ecclesiastes 4:9–12)*

God is Jealous

> *For you shall not worship any other god, for the Lord, whose name is Jealous, is a jealous God. (Exodus 34:14)*

God really does not want our life just so that we can say no to drugs. He doesn't want us serving Him to remain sober. He wants us because we have come to a realization of how much He loves us and forgives us as sinners, and in return, we start loving Him back. Once we realize this, we will want to live a life that's pleasing to God.

God is JEALOUS. This means exactly what you would think. God doesn't want us serving Him to be sober, to save our marriage, to keep from gambling, and so forth. He wants us serving Him because we love Him and appreciate who He is in our life. Serving and loving God guarantees us that we can live free from problems such as these—but this freedom is just a byproduct of our servitude.

God wants our entire life. If we withhold it, our love would be like that of the child who loves his parents just because they give him what he wants, or of the spouse who loves and is married because of her spouse's money. Those relationships are not healthy, and you do not get very many benefits from relationships founded on selfish motives. Likewise, if you love God for sobriety alone, your addictions will probably return.

God is a jealous God, and He wants us to surrender our entire life. He does not want us to pick and choose what parts of ourselves we want to give up.

You Are Fearfully and Wonderfully Made

> *I will give thanks to You, for I am fearfully and*
> *wonderfully made; wonderful are Your works, and*
> *my soul knows it very well. (Psalm 139:14)*

We all have a past. Our past will haunt us if we allow it to—that is not what God wants for us. He does not want us to feel condemned for the bad choices that we made prior to being redeemed. The bible tells us in Romans 8:1, "Therefore there is now no condemnation for those who are in Christ Jesus"

Christ has forgiven us, and we must believe this with our whole hearts or we will not be able to forgive ourselves. There is no amount of forgiveness from friends or family that can compare to Christ's all-encompassing and eternal forgiveness. Once we accept Christ's forgiveness, we will be able to forgive ourselves. It is not the forgiveness of men that will help us love and accept who we are in Christ but only the love of God; forgiveness comes "not by way of eyeservice, as men-pleasers, but as slaves of Christ, doing the will of God from the heart" (Ephesians 6:6).God created us a unique expression of Him, possessed of our own free will. As we grew up we exercised our free will, but our past does not change the unique, one-of-a-kind person that God created. This is why Christ came and sacrificed His life. God knew we were going to make some bad decisions and wanted a way to redeem us so that we could be that unique expression of Him again.

God does not want to change your personality—the essence of who He created you to be. He just wants you be the person He created re-deemed from the sin of the world, a new creation in Christ. Everyone was created with gifts and a personality like none other's, and God wants to use his gifts to us. He's not looking to change your DNA—just trans-form your sin into righteousness. Don't let the world, friends or family condemn you for your past. And especially do not condemn yourself. Latch on to God's forgiveness and love, for then and only then will you be able to forgive and love yourself.

No Complaining

There is a special spiritual blessing for those who do not complain, and a not-so-blessed flipside for those who do. For us to continue a positive, blessed walk with God, there is no room for complaining. Every day we need to enter into grateful, thanking God for all His new mercies.

> *The Lord is good to all, and His mercies are*
> *over all His works. (Psalm 145:9)*

I have seen over the years the effects of a negative outlook on life, and also those of having a positive outlook. The differences between the two are truly astounding. I rarely see someone go through our program suc-cessfully without giving his or her complaints to God.

Someone who came to God from a life of addiction must be careful in this area because when you start complaining, you display ingratitude God's other gifts. A habit of ingratitude will eventually lead you to bad decisions. God wants us to accept the leadership in our life. Whether you are in ministry or working at Wal-Mart, we all have leaders in our life, and God does not want us complaining against them.

Servants, be submissive to your masters with all respect, not only to those who are good and gentle, but also to those who are unreasonable. For this finds favor, if for the sake of conscience toward God a person bears up under sorrows when suffering unjustly. For what credit is there if, when you sin and are harshly treated, you endure it with patience? But if when you do what is right and suffer for it you patiently endure it, this finds favor with God. (1 Peter 2:18–20)

This was the apostle Peter's instructions to some Christian slaves—if anyone had reason to complain, they did. But Paul gave them instructions that if they wanted to continue in the favor of God, they must be submissive to harsh masters. When I think of this, I can't imagine any of us would ever fall into this category. If these were God's instructions to literal slaves, then what right do we have to complain in freedom? Complaining robs you of God's peace. It leads to worry and a poor attitude. God gives us great instructions on how to steer away from worry and complaining.

Finally, brethren, whatever is true, whatever is honorable, whatever is right, whatever is pure, whatever is lovely, whatever is of good repute, if there is any excellence and if anything worthy of praise, dwell on these things. The things you have learned and received and heard and seen in me, practice these things, and the God of peace will be with you. (Philippians 4:8–9)

Whenever you feel like complaining, stop and thank God for all He has done in your life: delivering you from addictions, divorce, gambling, and any other life-controlling problems. If we don't stop and choose to think about all the good that God has done, we will find ourselves in a bad spot. Choose to bless God and not complain against Him.

I will bless the Lord at all times; His praise shall continually be in my mouth. (Psalm 34:1)

Be Content for Safety

> *Remove far from me falsehood and lies; give me neither poverty*
> *nor riches; feed me with the food that is needful for me: Lest I be*
> *full, and deny thee, and say, Who is Jehovah? Or lest I be poor, and*
> *steal, and use profanely the name of my God. (Proverbs 30:8–9)*

There was a time I did not understand the concept of being content in any situation. I know I have not yet arrived, but at least now, I know that God has a plan for my life.

The apostle Paul told us that he had learned the art of being content in whatever situation he was in, which he demonstrated in the way he lived his life: "Not that I speak in respect of want: for I have learned, in whatsoever state I am, therewith to be content" (Philippians 4:11). I believe Paul's secret to contentment was his certainty of spending eternity with Christ.

Before knowing Christ, I chased after the things of this world only to wind up empty-handed. I only got temporary pleasure from drugs, drinking, and trivial fun. The world's fun is temporary. Just imagine if your happiness totally depended on your family, your job, your favorite hobby, or even your favorite sports team. Everything I have listed will fail you at some point, but God's love and His word never fail us.

Proverbs 30:8 states, "Give me neither poverty nor riches; feed me with the food that is needful for me." If you are walking with God and praying as this scripture states, then you can be assured that what God provides for you is exactly what you need and therefore you are able to remain content. Let us also look at verse 9: "Lest I be full, and deny thee, and say, Who is Jehovah? Or lest I be poor, and steal, and use profanely the name of my God." In other words, our deep concern and prayers must be focused on remaining true to God's plan for us, and continually asking God, "Give me what you want me to have." We can say to God,

1. You know me better than anybody else,

2. You know what I can handle,

3. You know how much wealth will puff me up with pride and forget You, and,

4. You know how little I can handle so that I would not do something illegal and forget You, as well.

The word of God tells us in 1 Timothy 6:6 that godliness with contentment is great gain. I can remember when I first came to Christ and literally had no material possessions. It was probably the most content time of my life. So it is a constant battle as we gain wealth, position, and fame to pray that God keeps us content and gives us exactly what we need. If we want great gain in our life and be able to walk in constant freedom, we must remain content where *there is safety.*

Ask Somebody

> *A man of understanding shall attain unto wise counsel. (Proverbs 1:5)*

After Christians have walked with Christ for some time, especially those who were once addicted, they face a common pitfall: Where the matters of daily life are concerned, they feel they do not need the counsel of other people anymore. Yet seeking wise counsel is a biblical principal, and one that does not change no matter how long you have walked with the Lord. A bad decision may lead us down a road that would have been avoided by asking somebody for their view.

I guess it's just a man-thing—that is, not being willing to pull the car over and ask for directions even when we are lost. We don't even like to read instructions. We just dump something out of its box and hope for the best.

There was a time I had the opportunity to buy a used Chevy Blazer wholesale. My intention was to resell it and make some extra money. I didn't pray about it, nor did I ask for anybody's opinion or advice. You see, I had worked in the car business for several years before I had given my life to Christ, and let's face it, we have a tendency to not ask advice or pray when dealing with things we are knowledgeable about. It's because of our pride. Well, I came to find out the hard way that the market on Chevy Blazers was really bad; this was right after Hurricane Katrina, and gas prices had soared. Had I asked somebody, I probably wouldn't have lost money on that deal.

I'm reminded of when the disciples had been fishing all night. Fishing was their profession. They took advice from Jesus, a preacher, teacher, and carpenter—not a commercial fisherman—and they went back out as He advised them, and they caught fish. It would behoove us to take advice from people whom God can use to make right decisions, even people not in our so-called profession. I learned a valuable lesson from that Chevy Blazer:

> Where no counsel is, the people fall; but in the multitude of counselors there is safety. (Proverbs 11:14)

Ask somebody!

You're the Apple of His Eye

> Keep me as the apple of the eye. (Psalm 17:8)

When I think of being the apple of God's eye, I am reminded of when I was struggling with my addiction. It was during one of my stays in a rehabilitation program. My mother was trying to describe to me how much my dad loved me, and it was breaking his heart to see me live the way I was living. She told me that I was the apple of his eye. Words cannot describe what that meant to me, and the saddest part of it was that no amount of my father's love was going to set me free from the sin that controlled my life. No amount of my love for him was going to set me free, either. I needed the love and grace of God.

Our main responsibility is to trust God.

Being the apple of someone's eye means that we are the center of his or her world. I believe we are the center of God's world. He wants the best for us, and I believe God trusts us! How does it feel to know that we are trusted by God? The bible tells us that God will trust us as we show ourselves faithful.

He who is faithful in a very little thing is
faithful also in much. (Luke 16:10)

One summer when I was probably about twelve years old, my dad took my brother and me to the lake. We were all going waterskiing. The day was going great. We had a good time skiing and swimming and boating. Then, to my surprise, my dad said that he wanted to ski. Well I'm thinking how is this going to happen? There is no one to drive the boat. My brother and I were too young, and the only time I had driven the boat was sitting in the seat with my dad. Then the words came: "Gary, I want you to pull me skiing." I was terrified and excited all at the same time. One thing my dad told me was to make sure and not let go of the steering wheel, because the boat pulls to the right. Well, here comes the moment when I am getting ready to pull my dad out of the water. I throttled the boat all the way, felt the resistance that you feel when you are jerking a skier out of the water, and I was dying to see if dad was up. I turned around to see if dad was up and as soon as I did, I let go of the steering wheel. The boat quickly turned to the right and was doing a 180-degree turn, and we were heading back towards my dad. As I watched, he let go of the rope and fell into the water. I thank God no one was hurt.

Likewise, we are the apple of God's eye.

The bible tells us in Luke 9:62, "But Jesus said to him, 'No one, after putting his hand to the plow and looking back, is fit for the kingdom of God.'" Realizing that we are the apple of God's eye and that He trusts us with great things will take us far. Our main responsibility is to trust Him in fulfilling His responsibility for our lives. We do that by not letting go of the steering wheel to look back. Just grab the wheel and go.

Be Driven by Eternity

But now being made free from sin and become
servants to God, ye have your fruit unto sanctification,
and the end eternal life. (Romans 6:22)

We have seen how secular treatment has no impact on our eternal destination. Therefore, being driven by thoughts of eternity will keep us on the narrow path of freedom and free of addiction.

We need to remind ourselves why we are on this journey. First of all, God made us free from sin to become a servant of His and to have a positive influence on the world around us. If we focus on having a positive influence and becoming a better person in Christ, we will help ourselves stay focused on eternity. The word of God tells us that "life is but a vapor," so let's face it—this short life of ours doesn't compare to eternity. Eternity will come when God does away with time. Where do you think our focus needs to be?

As we are praying for and modeling Christian behavior to our family and friends, our focus, drive, and motivation to win them to Christ should be on where they are going to spend eternity. Don't give too much time to their temporary problems, because those problems will begin to fade away as an individual walks with the Lord. If we could just get a glimpse of what eternity will be like, be it in heaven or hell, we would be motivated to win our family and friends to Christ.

Remember, fog will sometimes roll into our lives, and roll out again—but quitting is forever.

When I think about the thief on the cross and the pain that he endured, the one thing that gave him hope was that Jesus told him, "Today, you will be with me in paradise." We need to continually remind ourselves that is why we live the Christian life and that is why Christ died for us: eternal life.

I'm reminded of a statement I heard just the other day. If our life is a vapor, then that is not a long time to hang on and do the right thing.

> *And if thy hand or thy foot causeth thee to stumble, cut it off, and cast it from thee: It is good for thee to enter into life maimed or halt, rather than having two hands or two feet to be cast into the eternal fire. (Matthew 18:8)*

What Jesus is stressing here is the importance of eternity, and how driven we need to be while we are living this vapor of a life. The more we are focused on eternity, the more productive we will be; we will become better people in this life and be better witnesses to our friends and family.

There was a woman who swam from an island off the coast of California to the mainland; it was about the distance of swimming the English Channel. It was foggy on her attempt, and she could not see far ahead. She motioned for her boat to pick her up. She said she was tired. What she didn't realize was that she was almost there but she couldn't see the finish line because of the fog. She said, "If I had known it was that close, I could have made it." That is so much like our lives. Remember, fog will sometimes roll into our lives, and roll out again—but quitting is forever. We have no idea when time will cease in our lives and eternity will begin. Stay focused on what matters and you will not be tempted to get into the boat three feet short of the finish line: eternal life.

Speak No Russian

> *For in many things we offend all. If any man offend*
> *not in word, the same is a perfect man, and able*
> *also to bridle the whole body. (James 3:2)*

I have some very dear friends who live in the Altai region of Siberia, Russia. I have visited them several times. We work together with Teen Challenge to help people who are addicted to drugs and alcohol. These friends visited us in America for almost a month one summer. Whether they visit me or I visit them, however, we always need a translator to help us communicate. Yet there are short periods of time during our visits when the translator is not around, so we will communicate the best we can. It looks like we are playing charades, and so we laugh and really have a good time without being able to talk. It really is hilarious.

There was a time when they were visiting and I brought my friend, Genya, squirrel hunting. While we were hunting and communicating the best we could without a translator, I realized we had already spent a lot of time together and had not come close to upsetting each other. Not once did I think to myself, "I wonder what he meant by what he just said?" or, "He sounded upset." We definitely were not able to slander or gossip about anyone. Why? Because we couldn't communicate.

Oh, how awesome relationships in our lives would be if our communication were limited! We would not waste time on gossip, being a busybody, and slandering one another. In 1 Timothy 2:2, we are exhorted to "lead a quiet and peaceable life in all godliness and honesty."

Of our own free will, let us limit our speech so we do not offend our friends and family. The truth is, our tongue causes the most damage to relationships; and once the damage is done, the tongue is too weak to repair what's been damaged. If we offend someone or are offended ourselves, speech has brought on unnecessary drama and stress in our life. God wants us to "if possible, so far as it depends on you, be at peace with all men" (Romans 12:18). Living at peace with all men is just another spoke in the wheel that travels God's straight path.

Don't Get a Cosigner

> *But he forsook the counsel of the old men which they
> had given him, and took counsel with the young men
> that were grown up with him.* (*1 Kings 12:8*)

Let's say this in modern terms: "It's not a good thing to get your counsel from ya boys!"

The story that prompted this biblical advice was Rehoboam's search for counsel from some older wise men. These men had given him good counsel. Yet, as the bible tells us, he forsook their advice and sought a second opinion from some younger men, who basically told him what he wanted to hear.

This is never a good idea if you are trying to discern God's plan for your life. And for that matter, I think that Christians tend to get it confused; sometimes they concentrate so much on wanting to know God's plan for their life they do not focus on their personal walk with Christ. The most important thing is our personal walk, which is obedience to God's word. God's plan for us will fall into place.

Seek out older, wiser counsel that will tell you what you need to hear and not what you want to hear.

The bible tells us in Proverbs 11:14 "that there is safety in a multitude of counsel." This is where I believe many Christians today miss God's direction for their life and suffer for it, whether it be relationships, career moves, college, full-time ministry, and so forth. All of these decisions are major crossroads in our lives, and as a Christian, we should want God's perfect plan for our lives. That is why we chose to follow God, right? We want direction in our lives. Sometimes we get so comfortable with our walk with God that we start leaning on our own decisions. Proverbs 3:5 says, "Trust in the LORD with all thine heart; and lean not unto thine own understanding." Leaning on our own decisions really shouldn't be an option.

I have seen many people suffer unnecessary heartache as a result of following Rehoboam's example. They did not take counsel from the older and wiser people in their lives, and listened instead to younger friends. Those people were looking for a *cosigner* from friends who were no further along in the Lord than themselves. Instead, we need to go to the older and wiser in the Lord, and LISTEN! God will use these people to help us make right decisions.

The bible tells us that because Rehoboam did not follow wise counsel and instead looked for cosigners and found them, God left Rehoboam to his own folly.

When you are faced with major decisions in your life, seek out older, wiser counsel that will tell you what you *need* to hear and not what you *want* to hear. Go outside of your family and friends, because let's face it, they are the ones who will be more likely to cosign with you. Seek diverse wisdom.

Tell the Truth

> *A truthful witness saves lives, but he who utters lies is*
> *treacherous. In the fear of the Lord there is strong confidence,*
> *and his children will have refuge. (Proverbs 14:25–26)*

The whole world will remember Hurricane Katrina. Since my wife and I moved to north Louisiana, we were blessed to have tenants renting our home in Chalmette, Louisiana. This home still had a substantial mortgage on it, and the rent that we received was just enough to cover that cost. We knew God had called us to leave that home and were confident that God would keep tenants in the home so we could continue to pay our mortgage. After all, God had been faithful to provide for the first five years.

When Katrina hit, our home received four feet of water. Everything had to be gutted. Doing so would take at least $50,000. We didn't have the money and we didn't have flood insurance. We were sure that we were going to lose our home through foreclosure because there was no way we could fix it. But I had heard on the news there was a $26,000 grant through FEMA for which we were eligible because we didn't have flood insurance.

Our hopes were high and I was optimistic as I dialed the toll free number. It was true—we were eligible. The woman started asking me questions. "Is this your primary residence?" I froze. So many reasons were running through my mind for answering yes. It cost more than the mobile home we were in, it was on a slab and the mobile home was on wheels. I'll say yes, I thought, get the money, and then go live there a while. All these scenarios were ways for me to justify a lie. Yet I couldn't lie. I was mindful that "in the fear of the Lord there is strong confidence, and his children will have refuge."

I told her that it was not our primary residence, hoping it wouldn't matter. She told me, "We can't help you." My wife and I were very discouraged.

Two weeks later, I got a phone call from an oil company. The representative said their refinery had ruptured a tank during the flood, and there may be oil on our property. They scheduled a meeting with us. Not many days passed, and at the meeting, they gave us a check for $26,000. The exact amount I would have gotten if I had lied! This was no coincidence; this was God taking care of His children.

We were excited, but how were we going to rebuild our house with $26,000? My wife and I tithed on the money first, giving to some people in need, and then started to rebuild. God did with our $26,000 what He did with the fishes and loaves when He fed five thousand people. It miraculously multiplied. Our house was rebuilt—we didn't get behind on our bills, and we still own it today. God has continued to keep tenants in it so we can continue to do what He has called us to do. I believe with all my heart that if I had lied, the same amount of money received on a lie would not have accomplished nearly as much as the miracle of honest money . If we want God's blessing on our life we have to be people of integrity, tell the truth on our income tax return, and avoid deception in all areas of our lives. Fear God, tell the truth and He will see to it that His children will have refuge.

Don't Do It

For my yoke is easy, and my burden is light. (Matthew 11:30)

Once God has removed addictions from our life, now comes the lifelong journey of inviting Him to continue to remove our shortcomings. If we don't welcome the continued purging of the Holy Spirit, we will risk the danger of our old habits sneaking back into our life. Don't have a New-Year's-resolution mentality.

The once-addicted—or any Christian, for that matter—sometimes tends to rely on personal promises rather than God's word. This is when we decide to give up a habit that we do not want to carry around any longer. It could be cigarettes; it could be food. The founder of Teen Challenge and Times Square Church, Reverend David Wilkerson, once said, "Food is a legalized sedative; we turn to it when we are sad and we turn to it when we are happy." When in this New-Year's-resolution mentality, we turn to any secular source of advice that money can buy: a book with the latest diet, nicotine patches, and so forth. None of this, for the most part, will be long-lasting because we are relying on our own strength.

Instead, I want to encourage you to do is find out what God's word has to say about your resolution. If it's your temper, your habit of being stingy, your avoidance of family time, your gossiping, your neglect of reading the bible, or yes, even your addiction, entrust your success to God's word. The sure way to have a long-lasting change is to find out what He says about your difficulty, and then give it to Him! Matthew 11:30 ensures us that the yoke of Lord is light.

Another diet book, another patch from the drugstore, an anger management class, or even another AA meeting is a difficult burden for us to bear. We can't do it! Give your burden to God this New Year's, or any time of year. Walk in the freedom of Grace and all you have to do is make a daily, Christ-conscious decision to not return to the things that are displeasing to God.

Have Faith

> *Now faith is the substance of things hoped for, the evidence of things not seen. (Hebrews 11:1)*

Some of my friends and family from Alabama will know of a place called Chimney Rock, located on beautiful Lake Martin. At Chimney Rock there was a rope swing that I had swung on many times during my childhood, but there was a visit as an adult that I remember in particular.

I climbed up the hill and out onto the rock. You had to literally stand on the very edge to catch the rope as someone threw it to you. It was very high in the air, and once you made the decision to swing, there is no option of changing your mind midair because you would just swing back into the rocks. When you swung out over the water, you had to let go.

I stood there with the rope in my hand, clutching the ski handle tied on the end. Following the rope upward with my eyes to where it was tied on a pine limb, I noticed several different colors of rope knotted together. I had to have faith that the people who tied these ropes had secured them well—I was entrusting my life to their handiwork.

I really felt like God spoke to my heart when I was standing on that rock with that rope swing in my hand. He spoke to me, saying, "If you will have the faith in Me that you have in the people that secured this rope swing—people whom you have never met or seen—I will take you for the ride of your life!"

How true that was! I survived the plunge into the lake, and I have entrusted my life to God. He also told us in Matthew 17:20, "And Jesus said unto them, 'Because of your unbelief: for verily I say unto you, if ye have faith as a grain of mustard seed, ye shall say unto this mountain, remove hence to yonder place; and it shall remove; and nothing shall be impossible unto you.'" The reality is that we tend to have a lot more faith in things that we shouldn't, or things we don't even trust. If we just have faith in a loving God, He is ready to take us on the ride of our lives!

Be Thankful

At Thanksgiving, Americans gather and share their gratitude. I think about the people who do not live for God; yet on Thanksgiving, they are doing the will of God. If they only knew! If the unbeliever only knew that his or her gratitude, in those moments, is the will of God. Something supernatural happens in a person's life when he or she is thankful. You see, the bible tells us in 1 Thessalonians 5:16–18 to be thankful, for this is the will of God. The blessing in a person's life for being thankful is great; and so is the lack of blessing, happiness, and peace for ingratitude. The apostle Paul taught us that he learned this secret in Philippians 4:11: "For I have learned to be content whatever the circumstances."

No matter what time period, social climate, and circumstances we live in, those factors do not have to affect our personal lives if we insulate ourselves with gratitude. I have truly realized that focusing on one negative thing in our life is enough to draw our attention and gratitude away from the many, many blessings

> *Be thankful, and let it be known.*

God has given us. When that happens, we lose our peace. Paul tells us in Philippians 4:8 "Finally, brothers, whatever is true, whatever is noble, whatever is right, whatever is pure, whatever is lovely, whatever is admirable—if anything is excellent or praiseworthy—think about such things."

Let me encourage you to not wait till the end of November to be thankful. Do not delay doing the will of God. Let's continue to do the will of God every day of our life by being thankful. Let God know you are thankful for Him, and let those around you know you are thankful for their presence in your life.

I read a quote recently that said not expressing your gratitude towards someone is like receiving a gift and not opening it. How true! Be thankful, and let it be known.

Don't Envy

> *Do not fret because of those who are evil or be envious of those who do wrong. (Psalm 37:1)*

In this verse David is saying not to fret about those people who are prospering by doing the wrong thing. God reassures us that selfish prosperity is not the way to true happiness.

I had been serving God a little over a year. I was singing in the choir. I was involved in the worship team, and I desired a wife. During this time, there was a friend of mine who wasn't living for God, and I remember the day that he walked into church one Sunday morning with a beautiful girl whose father happened to be a pastor. That's what *I* wanted! A pastors' daughter!

Words cannot describe the emotions I felt when I saw him walk into church with her, knowing he wasn't living right. Thoughts went through my mind like, "God, why are you blessing him who is not serving You," and, "I feel like You don't care about me right now. I think I am going back into the world! At least then I can find a wife." These were some very immature thoughts, but I was not exactly a mature Christian at the time. I wanted answers from God on fairness. I sounded like a little kid griping about a coveted toy that his brother got instead.

The truth is, that is exactly how we can be with God at times, and you know how frustrating and hurtful it can be when one of your children is upset and they feel like they haven't been treated fairly. I can only imagine how it would make God feel knowing how much he loves us and how perfectly He knows what's best for us. In fact, verse 2 of Psalm 37 says "For like the grass they will soon wither," and then verses 3 and 4 tell us, "Trust in the LORD and do good; dwell in the land, and enjoy safe pasture. Take delight in the LORD, and he will give you the desires of your heart."

In the end, God provided me with a beautiful wife. The relationship I was envious of did not prosper. Likewise, God wants to give you the desires of your heart. You just have to trust Him and not waste days and years of your life envying what seems like unfair prosperity; without Christ, there is no true prosperity.

Be a Giver

> *And Samuel said, Hath the LORD as great delight in*
> *burnt offerings and sacrifices, as in obeying the voice of*

*the LORD? Behold, to obey is better than sacrifice, and
to hearken than the fat of rams. (1 Samuel 15:22)*

This was early in the development of Mount Grace Teen Challenge for Men. We were offering the second-phase program for Louisiana Teen Challenge, where we continued to help men after they had been in one of our other programs for at least four months.

We had not been living on the property long when I was searching for ways to raise money. I can remember walking the property and praying. I felt the Lord speak to my heart—He said to buy a chainsaw, take the men out to these properties where timber had been cut, cut up what the timber companies had left behind into firewood, and sell it.

I called our bookkeeper and asked her about purchasing a chainsaw for the ministry. Her response was that she was sorry, but we really didn't have the money at the time. After praying about it some more, I felt God speak to my heart and say that I should purchase it myself. Whoa, I thought, I don't think we have $300. But after thinking about it and talking to Sandy, we were able to come up with $300 to purchase this saw. It cost almost as much as my wife and I made in a week. But I do not remember it being a sacrifice, for just as the Scripture says, "to obey is better than sacrifice." We bought the chainsaw, and four months later, the ministry had brought in $26,000 selling firewood.

How many times do we ignore the still-small voice tugging at the part of our humanity that is generous, and ignore it? We really need to heed that voice. You can never go wrong sowing into the kingdom.

It wasn't but a few months later that the businessman that donated the property to Teen Challenge called me and wanted to meet with me. He said, "I want to give you and Sandy three thousand dollars." My first reaction was that he meant he wanted it to go to the ministry, and so I asked him for clarity. He got specific: "I do not want it to go to the ministry. I want it to go to you and Sandy." I could do nothing but cry. His gift was ten times the cost of the chainsaw—what a return on our investment! Some people may say that this is a coincidence, but I know that it was God's blessing.

Always be sensitive to the voice of God, because you never know what kind of investment tip He is giving you. God does not want your sacrifice—He wants your obedience, and there lies your blessing.

PSALM 23, A PRAYER FOR ADDICTS

The Lord Is My Shepherd (Psalm 23:1)

God's grace will aid us in dealing with any of life's issues, including addiction. Psalm 23 promises that *the Lord is your shepherd.* My prayer is that you have truly made the Lord your shepherd, no matter if you are someone who has struggled with addiction or a family member that is crying out for a loved one.

This is such a beautiful psalm. Its wonderful promises cannot be tapped unless the Lord is our shepherd. A shepherd is someone that watches over His flock, protects His flock from prey. Sheep are helpless, unintelligent animals that need to have a shepherd. We are often compared to them in the bible, which should tell us the importance of needing a shepherd in our life—someone who knows what is best for us, who knows how to keep us from harm's way, who protects us from temptations, and who shelters us from the pressures of this world

I Shall Not Want (Psalm 23:1)

If Jesus is truly our shepherd, He promises we will want for nothing. I can trust that all my needs will be provided for. I will never lack for anything.

He Makes Me Lie Down in Green Pastures (Psalm 23:2)

If the Lord is your shepherd, you will be blessed with the best that the world, His creation, has to offer. He wants you to have lush, green pastures—not pastures that are parched and barren. He wants you to have everything you need and be comfortable.

He Leads Me Beside Quiet Waters (Psalm 23:2)

If the Lord is your shepherd, He promises you divine peace in the midst of anything that life may throw at you. God does not want his children living a life of stress and anxiety, struggling to survive a raging river. He wants us calm and able to deal with life peaceably. He will lead you to a calm way of living.

He Restores My Soul (Psalm 23:3)

If the Lord is your shepherd then He has restored you, made you anew, and given you a new way of living.

Think of the way a car is restored to what it once was. We cannot look at everyone else around us that have been restored by God, and expect that God is going to give us the exact same paint job, the same interior, and so forth. He has a special restoration plan for each individual, because each person is unique. We are all going to have the same character and righteousness, but God has a special restoration process for you. He has a different spouse, job, home, car, and location for you, and none of it is going to be like another person's. If the Lord is your shepherd, He has a special restoration process designed for you—not just rehabilitation.

He Guides Me in the Paths of Righteousness for His Name's Sake (Psalm 23:3)

If the Lord is your shepherd, He will take you down a path of right living. Even when you don't know what right living is, He will guide you by His spirit. God's word tells us that the law of God is written on our hearts even before we are saved

> *in that they show the work of the Law written in their*
> *hearts, their conscience bearing witness. (Romans 2:15)*

So even before we start following Christ, we have a sense of what is right and wrong. Once we accept that Jesus shed His blood for the remission of our sins, then we are led to a path of righteousness; a path of right living for His name's sake.

God has an agenda—not only does He love and care about you, but He wants to lead you down a path of right living so that you will bring glory to His name and lead others to His light.

Even Though I Walk Through the Valley of the Shadow of Death, I Fear No Evil, for You Are with Me (Psalm 23:4)

We are going to experience tough times. It's not a matter *if* we do; it's just a matter of *when* we do. We will experience death, sickness, offense, evil, and slander. If the Lord is our shepherd, we are promised guidance through these times. We will not live in fear of when these times may come, but neither will we fear in their midst.

Your Rod and Your Staff, They Comfort Me (Psalm 23:4)

If the Lord is our shepherd, we have the comfort of knowing that God is going to use situations in life to teach us. He may discipline us with the conviction of the Holy Spirit, and sometimes He may use people or authorities to discipline us—but it's because He loves us.

If the Lord is our shepherd, this is not something to dread or complain about. As a follower of Christ directed by His rod and staff, this is a comfort.

You Prepare a Table Before Me in the Presence of My Enemies (Psalm 23:5)

Your enemy could be anything. It may be alcohol, cocaine, or any other type of drug. It could be gambling or any other problem that is an enemy to prevent you from experiencing a blessed life. If the Lord is your shepherd, He will make you a champion over your enemies and prepare a table for you that represents victory and blessings in your life.

You Have Anointed My Head with Oil; My Cup Overflows (Psalm 23:5)

If the Lord is your shepherd, He has a special anointment for you. He will anoint you for service. He will give you all the power you need to be a model of what God has done in your life. All of us who have been restored by God's grace now have the ministry of restoration to serve, and God will equip you to be successful in this for His name's sake.

Surely (Psalm 23:6)

The meaning of *surely* in the Greek is certainly, absolutely. So whatever God is about to tell us next, you can count on it.

Goodness and Loving-kindness Will Follow Me All the Days of My Life (Psalm 23:6)

If the Lord is your shepherd, He is working everything out in your life. He wants you to have a good life, one that is abundant in forgiveness, comfort, joy, righteousness, holiness, power, might, strength, favor, prosperity, success, promotion, and everything else that is good on earth and heaven shall follow you and remain with you all the days of your life.

And I Will Dwell in the House of the LORD *Forever (Psalm 23:6)*

If the Lord is your shepherd, you have the assurance of eternal life. You have the promise of an abundant life here on earth, and eternity in Heaven. Let the words of this psalm be a part of your life. Make the Lord the shepherd over every area of your life. He wants to be your Lord—He wants Kingship. Let Him have His rightful place, and you will take hold of all the things He has promised for His children.

CONCLUSION

If you have considered yourself an addict, there is hope. At Teen Challenge, we are usually the last resort for a lot of people. Most of the people who are in our programs have been to secular rehabs multiple times. We are a last resort because people tend to put more faith in something that costs a lot of money rather than turn to something that is free. Well, the Gospel is free! And it will free the person who has faith that its message is true.

God loves you. A better life is waiting for you, and it is just one decision away—a decision to surrender your life to Christ. He wants control not only of your addictions, but your life. Giving my life over to God was the single greatest event of my life. Not only did the Gospel free me from desiring drugs and alcohol, but freed me to live life. The enemy tried to destroy my life, but Jesus gave me an abundant life. That life is for everyone who chooses to accept the Gospel by faith.

The thief comes only to steal and kill and destroy; I came that
they may have life, and have it abundantly. (John 10:10)

Let us not lose heart in doing good, for in due time we
will reap if we do not grow weary. (Galatians 6:9)

If you are on the road to freedom, I want to encourage you to be patient and remain humble. Do not try to restore and repair at once everything that took you years to damage. It was about two years after I had been serving God that my brother approached me about dedicating his first born, Abbie. Understand that I had tried to restore my brother's relationship when I graduated Teen Challenge, and it seemed like the more I tried, the worst it got. So I stopped trying and started trusting God. After I gave it to God, that is when the relationship started being restored. What a privilege to dedicate Abbie to the Lord! It was especially so, knowing that Matt hadn't had an older brother in his life for many years. I had abandoned him, and he was rightfully bitter especially after our brother Randy had died. God restored our relationship in God's time, and His timing is perfect. Be patient and don't try to fix everything. Just apply Matthew 6:33 to your life: "But seek first His kingdom and His righteousness, and all these things will be added to you."

> *Therefore humble yourselves under the mighty hand of God,*
> *that He may exalt you at the proper time, casting all your*
> *anxiety on Him, because He cares for you. (1 Peter 5:6–7)*

✝

If you are a family member, believe that your loved one will change. God is very concerned about every one of his children, and His heart is breaking alongside yours.

> *I have decided to deliver such a one to Satan for the*
> *destruction of his flesh, so that his spirit may be saved*
> *in the day of the Lord Jesus. (1 Corinthians 5:5)*

This passage of scripture as it is reads sounds very harsh—*turn someone over to Satan*. But Satan represents the world. Paul understood there were people that needed to be beaten up by the world some more so that they would reach a place of repentance.

I pray that if you're loved one is not showing signs of improvement, you are willing to tell God, "Whatever it takes short of death for the sake of their soul, I am ready, and I will not get in the way of the consequences that may bring about repentance." My parents went through seventeen sleepless years of torment. I know how hard it is, but God loves us and wants us to let go and let Him take care of it.

> *And we know that God causes all things to work*
> *together for good to those who love God, to those who are*
> *called according to His purpose. (Romans 8:28)*

CONTACT INFORMATION AND RESOURCES

CONTACT THE AUTHOR

Gary Bentley
570 Braxton Road
Dodson, Louisiana 71422
504-481-5499
garyjamesbentley@gmail.com

LOUISIANA TEEN CHALLENGE CENTERS

MOUNT GRACE TEEN CHALLENGE FOR MEN (*second phase*)
564 Braxton Rd. Dodson, LA 71422
318-648-2426

NEW ORLEANS TEEN CHALLENGE FOR MEN (*first phase*)
1905 Franklin Ave. New Orleans, LA 70117
504-947-7949

SHREVEPORT TEEN CHALLENGE FOR MEN (*first phase*)
452 Stoner Ave Shreveport, LA 71101
318-673-8383

RUSTON TEEN CHALLENGE FOR MEN (*first phase*)
411 E. California Ave. Ruston, LA 71270
318-254-2830

MOUNT GRACE TEEN CHALLENGE FOR WOMEN
(*first and second phase*)
560 Deer Pen Rd. Winnfield, LA 71483
318-648-1100

MINDEN TEEN CHALLENGE WOMEN AND CHILDREN CENTER
1528 Evergreen Rd, Minden, LA 71055
318-648-0203

For information on Teen Challenge Centers around the country, go to
WWW.TEENCHALLENGEUSA.COM

CPSIA information can be obtained at www.ICGtesting.com
Printed in the USA
LVOW11s1233130614

389923LV00001B/1/P